SUE HAASLER started her blog pause
weekly reviews of *Holby City* are read l
This led to a meeting with the show's p
here the idea of a book started to take

Sue lives in London. Her publishe
and *Two's Company*, which was optioned for film by Warner Brothers.
Her new novel *Half A World Away* will be published in 2018 by The
Dome Press.

For more information visit www.pauseliveaction.wordpress.com.

HOLBY CI✝Y

BEHIND THE SCREEN

SUE HAASLER

SilverWood

Published in 2018 by SilverWood Books

SilverWood Books Ltd
14 Small Street, Bristol, BS1 1DE, United Kingdom
www.silverwoodbooks.co.uk

ISBN 978-1-78132-562-9 (paperback)
ISBN 978-1-78132-786-9 (ebook)

British Library Cataloguing in Publication Data
A CIP catalogue record for this book is available from
the British Library

Page design and typesetting by SilverWood Books
Printed by TJ International on responsibly sourced paper

CONTENTS

ON THE SCREEN

INTRODUCTION

We all love being here. That's why we do what we do. – *David Ames*

Holby City has been on our screens since 1999, for much of that time being shown fifty-two weeks of the year. It's consistently one of the BBC's highest-rated shows.

It's quite an achievement to produce that much television year in, year out, and to keep doing it to such a first-class standard. The evidence of Holby's quality is there on our screens every week, but the more I found out about the sheer amount of thought, creativity, skill, hard work and attention to detail that goes into every single episode, the more impressed I became. A lot of seriously talented people work for Holby, each with their individual area of expertise. The amount of organisation to get this to function is mind-boggling, but the remarkable thing about it is how relaxed everything feels. People are so tuned in to what they need to be doing that there doesn't seem to be any panic or stress. There's a lot of laughter, and as I talked to people, the phrase I heard again and again was, "It's just like a family".

One explanation for Holby's success, and why Tuesday at 8pm is essential viewing for so many people, is the consistently high quality of the writing and the acting. Writers are strongly encouraged to develop the script in their own way, and the emphasis is on sharp, witty dialogue. The show attracts the finest actors either in long-running roles or as guests. The guest-star roster on its own is a who's who of British acting talent.

And it's set in a hospital. The main characters are doctors and surgeons—in some ways, incredible beings with the power of life and death in their hands (and don't some of them know it). In many other ways, as fallible and human as everybody else. Meanwhile they're dealing with people who are at a crisis point in their lives. It's a heightened atmosphere and a background for engrossing drama.

Holby City was originally conceived by Tony McHale and Mal Young as a spin-off from the BBC's long-running Saturday night medical drama *Casualty*. The two programmes are set in the same hospital in the fictional city of Holby, although they're filmed 160 miles apart—*Casualty* in Cardiff (and previously in Bristol) and Holby in Borehamwood in Hertfordshire.

Casualty's storyline focuses each week on one or two particular patients and their stories. By the end of the episode the guest stories are generally resolved, giving each episode a self-contained feel. *Holby City* is much more about the regular characters, with the guest characters serving to move the regulars' stories on as much as to provide a story themselves. I always think if *Casualty* is linked short stories, Holby is a novel.

The first episode of *Holby City* premiered on 12 January 1999. 'Whose Heart Is It Anyway?' was written by Tony McHale, and the cast included Michael French as Nick Jordan, George Irving as Anton Meyer, Angela Griffin as Jasmine Hopkins and Nicola Stephenson as Julie Fitzjohn. Of the current cast, the longest-serving is Hugh Quarshie (Ric Griffin), who joined in 2001 at the start of Series 4.

For the purposes of this book, I decided to concentrate on current characters and recent storylines. The history of a programme that has run for eighteen years and over 800 episodes, with more than 100 regular cast members, would take a book in itself, and I still wouldn't be able to cover everything and please everyone.

As it is, because Holby is nonstop and filming continues every week of the year apart from two weeks at Christmas, it's unavoidable that this book will be at least a little bit out of date before you even get to read it. During the few weeks I spent at Holby interviewing people for the book, executive producer Oliver Kent became head of continuing drama series for BBC Studios; series producer Simon Harper became executive producer of *Holby City* and *Casualty*; and story producer Kate Hall stepped into Simon's old role to be series producer. Some planned storylines changed considerably between my first visits in late 2016 and the bulk of my visits in spring 2017, with actors such as Chizzy Akudolu (Mo Effanga), Lucinda Dryzek (Jasmine Burrows) and Camilla Arfwedson (Zosia March) moving on to pastures new after their Holby success, and new storylines and characters constantly being devised and developed. So the best I can do is present a snapshot of the work that goes into the programme and the incredibly talented, caring and committed people who work week in, week out to bring us such brilliant entertainment.

Note: Whenever an episode is cited, the series and episode number will be given as, for example, 18/35 – meaning Series 18, episode 35.

HOLBY IS A PLACE

When I started here I was overwhelmed by the
sheer size of this place. – *James Anderson*

Holby City Hospital really is a place, but it isn't really a hospital. The building you see in the exterior (and a lot of the interior) shots is called Neptune House, and it's part of the BBC Elstree complex which also houses the *EastEnders* set. So you could say that Holby is right next door to Walford (though its ED department is in Cardiff, where *Casualty* has been filmed since moving from Bristol in 2011).

Neptune House was built in 1961 as an office block for ATV Studios, and over the years the iconic L-shaped building has appeared in a variety of televisual guises—viewers of a certain age might recognise it as the entrance to the school in *Grange Hill*, or the headquarters of top-secret alien-fighting organisation SHADO in the 60s cult sci-fi series *UFO*.

When you walk up to the building for the first time, you immediately notice that it looks just like a hospital. The windows bear the Holby City NHS logo and there's hospital signage in the car park. The inside has a familiar feeling, too, especially the staircases which are often used for scenes in the show. If the lift should open on the third floor as it takes you up to the Holby production offices on the fifth floor, (with that familiar 'lift going up' message), what you see in front of you is frosted glass with 'Keller Ward' etched on it. It's quite a strange sensation at first, and even stranger when someone in scrubs wanders by.

The original Holby set was what is now the Darwin set on the sixth floor of Neptune House. Originally the set was divided in two, with Darwin at one side and Keller at the other. Now, as befits the country's leading fictional CT facility, Darwin has the whole space to itself and looks impressively high-tech and glossy. Apart from the main space surrounding the nurses' station, there are various other rooms, including Jac Naylor's office. When I visited I was worried to see a member of the crew casually sitting at Jac's desk. It was so familiar from the show that I expected her to storm in with a withering comment. (Rosie Marcel was at that moment in the main part of the 'ward' running through a walk-and-talk scene with Chizzy Akudolu). Whatever spaces aren't going to be in shot are used to house any equipment that isn't in use on standby until it's needed. In another space the director, the script supervisor and others will be watching the images the camera is capturing. Makeup artists will be sitting next to their boxes of kit, ready to apply any touch-ups to the actors as needed, and if any major prosthetics are being used there'll also be someone from that department to keep an eye on them.

The theatres are equipped with all the up-to-date tech you'd see in a genuine operating theatre, and an actual, qualified theatre nurse ensures that each theatre is set up in an authentic way with the surgical instruments, swabs etc arranged exactly as they would be for actual surgery (and specific to the operation being depicted). The operating theatre lights are just the same as you'd see in a modern operating theatre.

Keller, on the third floor, looks like a real hospital ward, albeit one with a lot of TV equipment stashed in every spare room and cupboard. Keller is a more difficult space to film in because of the layout. Director Jermain Julien described it as a "tube," and directors have to be creative to make shots in Keller look as interesting as possible.

This is where it gets complicated. While Holby's doctors and nurses might get from Keller to AAU or Pulses via a quick trip in the lift or jogging down the stairs, in reality you have to walk quite a long way to get there. AAU is at the other end of the site, in a connected but separate building, in what's known as the Scenery Block. It's a purpose-built set, so the 'walls' you see on AAU are flats—stage scenery mounted on a frame. You probably haven't noticed, but there's no natural daylight there either, which apparently makes it a disorienting experience to film in there for a whole day, with no idea whether it's light or dark, raining or sunny outside. On the other hand, it's a flexible space, which makes it easier to work in, and some people say for that reason they prefer working in AAU to the other sets.

The long corridor with the arched sides where you'll often have a walk-and-talk scene is known as the Victorian Corridor and is a bit misleading. It looks like the oldest part of the hospital, but like the rest of AAU it's just a set. The camera can never look up, because there's no ceiling where you'd expect one to be, so you can't have any of those patient's-view scenes from a trolley as lights flash past overhead. And then there's the staircase at the end, the one with a vending machine at the bottom, the place of choice if Hanssen needs to make a stirring speech to the troops. There's no point going up those stairs, because it's a dummy staircase that only leads to a dead end at the top.

After work, there's nothing the Holby staff like better than a nice, refreshing beverage, so they head to Albie's. You don't often see Henrik Hanssen in Albie's, but if he ever fancied a drink he could be there in no time as the sets for Hanssen's office and Albie's are back-to-back on a former music stage. Again, the 'walls' of these are flats.

Rather poignantly, on Hanssen's desk when I visited was a folder that still bore the name of his old unrequited love, Sahira Shah. I wondered whether he'd hung onto it for sentimental reasons. Like AAU, Hanssen's office has no natural daylight and the view from his window is actually printed onto a piece of scenery that's propped up on the other side of his 'window'. It's never specified where in the building Hanssen's office is, but the photograph on the translite (backdrop) that forms his view is the same as the view from the fourth floor, which is where the design department is. Everything else is done by clever lighting.

Talking of lighting, Albie's and Hanssen's office weren't in use when I was there, and the atmosphere was cold and a bit eerie. There are no windows and the office has a subterranean feel to it. The fireplace and tartan armchairs in Albie's were familiar, but it was missing the warm lighting and cosy touches that make it look like a real bar. The set is usually dressed with glasses, and there were menus on the tables advertising such delights as the Albie's Relaxer (£6) and the appropriate but maybe slightly bad-taste Morphine Drip at £7. What you actually see the cast drinking is always fruit juice or water.

While the alcohol might not be real, the famous muffins in Pulses certainly are, which is lucky for the crew because they get to eat them when they've finished filming. Pulses is another purpose-built set, and it's surrounded by other usable areas such as a pharmacy.

Behind the counter at Pulses there's a door. You might imagine that it leads to the cupboard where all the lovely muffins are kept, but it serves a different purpose. Brace yourself—the much-used and often-seen lift in the reception area isn't a lift at all. It doesn't go anywhere and doesn't even move. The doors are opened and closed by a winding mechanism, which is in that cupboard in Pulses. So when you see the lift doors opening and closing, there's someone out of shot cranking them, and the proper lift sounds are added later in post-production.

Other sets are built as and when needed. The set for the flat that used to be shared by Dominic, Digby and Zosia was taken down and in its place the set for Isaac Mayfield's flat was being built when I visited, with much hammering and sawing going on. Other rooms can be temporarily dressed for a particular use, for example Mr T's office, but then used for something else like a psychiatrist's office at other times. Detailed photographs are taken of each set so they can be reproduced at a future time if necessary.

Apart from the Keller and Darwin sets, the other sets are accessed from a very long corridor. This corridor is the home to the prosthetics, makeup and costume departments, and also houses dressing rooms. Post-production is also based in that part of the building, and as well as Holby, *EastEnders* have some of their post-production there, *Strictly Come Dancing* also has offices and there's a studio which is used for visiting productions.

Because it's a shared building, it means that any filming in the corridors, staircases, gardens, car parks and the notorious roof has to be treated as location filming. Holby has a location manager who has to organise filming in the communal areas. Although the Holby signage is usually in place in the car park, when they aren't filming there it's used as a normal car park for people working in the building. The garden area, where so much drama has taken place over the years, is more often used in the summer for people to sit and eat their lunch. When I visited in September they were filming Christmas episodes and there was a Christmas tree there, but by Christmas itself all that had gone and the garden was looking damp and gloomy in the fog that hung around Borehamwood all day.

I can't help thinking of the garden as the Linden Cullen Memorial Shrubbery. Linden Cullen (played by Duncan Pow) was killed at the end of series 12 when he was cracked over the head with a vodka bottle wielded by a heroin addict patient in the garden.

It's not the only dramatic incident to have taken place in Holby's outdoor spaces over the years. It's seen the wedding of Oliver Valentine and Tara Lo (15/26 'Promises, Promises,' by Nick Fisher and Dana Fainaru) and was where Jonny Maconie proposed to girlfriend Bonnie (16/22 'Exit Strategy Part 1' by Robert Goldsbrough) and where Morven Shreve proposed to Arthur Digby (18/24 'Who You Are' by Patrick Homes).

It's also the last resting place of Serena Campbell's mother Adrienne, whose ashes were buried there by Serena and Raf (17/7 'Flesh and Blood' by Jamie Crichton). "I'm glad she's somewhere I can see her all the time," Serena said, telling Raf, "You're going to have to help me stop the drunks peeing on her."

The garden has been the scene of many poignant moments. In 17/10 ('Star of Wonder' by Julia Gilbert), a very ill Zosia became fixated on the idea that a patient was her late mother. Later Zosia found herself looking for her mother under the Christmas tree in the garden.

There was high drama in 17/41 ('Family Fortunes' by Joe Ainsworth), when Digby spotted a seemingly lifeless hand protruding from the shrubbery. We were led to believe the hand belonged to Mo Effanga because her father Clifford had become embroiled with some Very Nasty Men. In a twist, though, it wasn't Mo but her sister (or, biologically-speaking, cousin) Adele who ended up being bludgeoned in the bushes, by someone who couldn't tell one Effanga from the next.

It was only natural that there should be some kind of memorial to Arthur Digby in Holby's best-used outdoor space. In 18/43 ('Back in the Ring' by Jeff Povey), Ric Griffin unveiled a plaque in his honour, which was wonky and cheap-looking. Ric wasn't satisfied that this was a fitting tribute, and decided to set up the Arthur Digby Foundation, to seek out new medical talent wherever it might manifest itself. The little wonky plaque still remains as a permanent visual reminder.

As well as the memorials to dearly departed characters, there are two benches in the garden in memory of sadly missed members of the Holby family. One bench is dedicated to Ron Pinches. Ron was a member of the post-room team, and after his death the bench was placed opposite the room where he used to work.

Laura Sadler played nurse Sandy Harper from 2000 until her tragic accidental death in 2003 at the age of just twenty-two. Line producer Lynn Grant said that, for Holby, Laura's death was "unbelievable pain, it was a shutdown, it was hard to even think". Eventually they were able to talk to Laura's mum about how to write Laura's much-loved character of Sandy out of the show. Between them, they decided to give her a happy ending in which she won the lottery and moved to Australia. Meanwhile, the bench in the garden, which can be seen in some scenes, is a lasting memorial to her. It's inscribed, 'To Laura, with love from Holby City'.

CASUALTY CROSSOVERS

Some people think we film *Holby* down in Bristol and I point
out that not even *Casualty* is there any more. – *Ali Liddle*

Many *Holby City* fans are also fans of *Casualty* and a frequent grumble
is that the two programmes, although set in the same fictional universe,
sometimes seem like they're hardly related. To take one example: *Casualty*
staff do their after-work drinking in the pub on the corner, but you never
see staff from the rest of the hospital there. *Holby City*'s off-duty doctors
and nurses prefer the luxury of Albie's.

Oliver Kent, who was executive producer of both shows from 2013-
2017, says it's important that each show is a distinct brand, because that
strengthens each show and justifies their existence as separate entities.

Fans of both shows enjoy it when they cross over, although it takes
a lot of work to make that happen. The most obvious reason for that is that
Casualty is made in Cardiff (previously Bristol) and *Holby City* is made
in Hertfordshire. There are the practicalities of the actors travelling, and
making room in the schedule when an actor isn't needed for filming in their
own show and can be available to go and work in the other. It's not only
the physical distance that's a consideration, though. Keeping the *Casualty*
and *Holby City* worlds running nicely in parallel is a very complicated task.

If a big event happens in one of the shows, it needs to be referenced in the other (otherwise viewers of both will start saying, "How come they never mentioned...?"). When paramedic Jeff died on *Casualty* in October 2014, it would have been strange not to have mentioned it on the sister show, particularly as Fletch had only recently moved from the ED (*Casualty*) to work in AAU (*Holby City*). The story departments of the two shows therefore always know what's happening in each other's stories.

A tricky consideration is that *Holby City* appears regularly, pretty much every Tuesday, fifty-two weeks a year. Because *Casualty* is screened on Saturday nights, it's often replaced by sports and events like *The Eurovision Song Contest*. This can put it out of synch with whatever's happening on *Holby*.

Connie Beauchamp's car went over a cliff in the *Casualty* episode that aired on 30 July 2016 and the accident was, literally, a cliffhanger for the end of their series 30. Series 31 started with the thirtieth anniversary hour-long special where a helicopter crashed into the ED. In *Casualty's* fictional world these events happened on the same day. In reality, the Olympic Games in Brazil meant the helicopter crash episode didn't air until 27 August—four weeks after Connie's car had gone off the cliff. Holby had had four episodes in that time, so a bit of suspension of disbelief was required.

The helicopter crash and its aftermath was shot in Cardiff in May 2016, while the related *Holby City* episodes were filmed in June. The Holby team were able to watch a rough edit of what *Casualty* had done with the helicopter crash, so they could understand what had happened in the story. They also used some of *Casualty's* footage in the 'Previously...' section, to introduce the episode to Holby fans who might not have seen the relevant *Casualty* episode. Not only did they have to show the crash, but also introduce the character of Steph, who was initially a *Casualty* character but would later be part of the storyline where Fletch was stabbed with a screwdriver on *Holby City*.

For continuity purposes, the injuries on Connie Beauchamp's face had to be reproduced exactly from the *Casualty* episode when she came in to Holby. It was a complicated makeup and so the makeup artist who worked on it for *Casualty* came to Borehamwood to recreate it perfectly.

The *Casualty* helicopter crash episode aired on the Saturday, with the aftermath following seamlessly on Holby the following Tuesday. There was a tiny hiccup in that the Holby script mentioned that four people had died in the helicopter crash, whereas *Casualty* had it as eight. It was filmed with someone saying "four" on Holby, and this had to be fixed later in post-production.

There could have been a lot more trouble if something had happened to the schedule on the Saturday night and *Casualty* hadn't been able to go out as planned. Holby wouldn't have been able to air their episode without completely ruining the drama of the *Casualty* episode, and Holby's episode was an important one as it started off the storyline about Fletch's traumatic injuries and his slow recovery, as well as being the episode where Bernie and Serena had their first kiss in the aftermath of saving Fletch's life in theatre.

BEHIND THE SCENES

EXECUTIVE PRODUCER AND SERIES PRODUCER: OLIVER KENT AND SIMON HARPER

We brush the ice and hope it goes in the
right direction we want it to. – *Oliver Kent*

Everyone I talked to at Holby obviously loved the work they did and the phrase, "It's like a family", cropped up over and over. One of the Holby staff said to me, "If you interview anyone in TV they'll all say everyone's lovely, but what you have to look for is whether their eyes are smiling when they say it." At Holby, the smiles all look sincere.

If the atmosphere and tone of a workplace is set by the people in charge, it's quite obvious why Holby is such a nice place to work. At the time of this interview (in September 2016) Oliver Kent was the executive producer of *Holby City* and *Casualty*. In December 2016 he became head of continuing drama series for BBC Studios with oversight of *EastEnders*, *Doctors* and *River City* too. Simon Harper was the series producer of Holby, but has since moved to be executive producer.

They are both warm, approachable people, who are incredibly passionate about the success and quality of Holby, and work together so well that talking to them is like talking to a double act. They sometimes even finish each other's sentences.

Simon describes Ollie's role as being "the BBC quality controller".

Ollie says, "I have to make sure I've got the right people in place on Holby and *Casualty* to make them the best they can be, the best written they can be, and make sure they come in on budget and that they deliver a big audience."

The two of them have an excellent working relationship and say they're on the same wavelength editorially, though Simon jokes that he tends towards darker storylines ("Miserable and bleak," jokes Ollie. "But sardonically witty," corrects Simon). The important point is that they would never approve a story that the other didn't believe in.

It's Simon's job (now Kate Hall's) to manage the actors on a day-to-day basis ("Not that the actors take much managing, because they're delightful") and he reads every draft of every script. Both of them watch the daily assemblies—a reel of what's been shot the day before. This is a chance for either of them to pick up on things they're particularly pleased with or to spot potential problems.

Simon says that the job of producer is to have a vision of what you want in terms of tone and story, and to enable the execution of that vision. This includes "hiring the right people, communicating what you want, and empowering those people to be able to turn out what you want." Ollie describes it like the sport of curling. "You know how they brush the ice? We brush the ice and hope it goes in the right direction we want it to."

Having an overview also helps them to see if there's anything missing. "It could be about the diversity of the cast, it could be have we got enough nurses, have we got the loveable character, have we got the older, wiser figure of the hospital, have we got the villain," says Simon.

At Holby at any one time they'll have episodes in various stages of development from what's going out that week to about a year ahead. Simon says with experience it becomes second nature and isn't as confusing as it sounds, although Christmas is a bit strange. "*Casualty* did Christmas in July," says Ollie. "We were doing it in September and then real Christmas comes around and you think, 'Haven't we had Christmas?' But of course we haven't, it's just been telly Christmas, fake Christmas."

Simon says they try to look after their team as much as possible. "What I always say about Holby is you're making a quality drama, an hour a week, and it's shot on single camera, filmically. It's an hour of proper, grown-up, complex drama, but you're delivering it in soap quantities, and we never stop. Obviously we all get holidays, but it's only for two weeks every Christmas that the whole machine shuts down. There's no getting away from the fact that it's stressful. It's wonderful, I've done it for ten years now and you couldn't give up the burst of adrenaline and even the occasional stress. It becomes second nature and it works well, but my point is it's tough enough without having egos or disrespect."

"We have to make it the best possible experience for the people doing it," Ollie says, "And I think on the whole we manage it."

From the actors' point of view, they try to make working on the show have the feel of a traditional rep company. "More than most companies of actors you could ever find, they're all really plugged into their characters and they're always on this corridor all the time talking about what they've got coming up," says Ollie. "We allow them to influence what's coming up as far as is possible and realistic, and that really pays dividends."

Acting on Holby involves long hours of intense work and it would be easy for people to become burned out. To stop that happening, Ollie and Simon try to accommodate requests for a break if the actors want to pursue other projects. Hugh Quarshie (Ric Griffin) took a break to play the lead in *Othello* at the RSC, and was temporarily written out. "Ric's daughter Jess being out somewhere in the world is usually a good reason for Ric to be away, but Verona Joseph wasn't available so we restoried with Ric's granddaughter Darla and son Kofi," says Simon. When Bernie Wolfe went abroad for a few weeks just after she and Serena first got together, this was to accommodate a request for time off from Jemma Redgrave. She loved the role, but needed a break. Situations like this are treated as story opportunities anyway, in this case breaking the pair up and leaving viewers worrying whether that was the end of the 'Berena' story. Similarly, the storyline about Serena's daughter was partly developed to give Catherine Russell the opportunity to take time off, while at the same time being a powerful story in itself.

It's the nature of the profession that, no matter how much they enjoy a job, actors will sometimes want to pursue other opportunities. Oliver Kent remembers when Paul Bradley (Elliot Hope) told them he was leaving. "I flatly refused to believe him, and he gave us about a year and a half's notice," he says. "We did everything we could do to persuade him not to go."

A character Ollie would really like to see return is Michael Spence, played by Hari Dhillon. "He had this incredible swagger and energy that no other character has yet matched," he told me. "We've got brilliant characters, but there's something so distinctive about Michael Spence. We never ran out of stories for him. We never tried to soften him, we never tried to explain why he did as he did."

Simon admits that before he joined Holby in 2006 he didn't have the best impression of the show. "I wrongly perceived it as faintly trashy," he says. "I had no idea what went into these shows and what they really were." He changed his mind after watching about fifteen episodes. Starting as a script editor he worked his way up, always being very closely involved in the editorial side and the script process.

"I joined when Tony McHale was the executive producer, and also the lead writer," he says. "The show owes Tony so much. He kept up with the changing times and put it on single camera and gave it its current filmic quality. He changed the pace of it—he showed us endless episodes of *The West Wing* at the time, for aspiration of tone and keeping it on the move much more. Tony was obsessed with *The West Wing* and all the stylised stuff he was into, which I also loved, like flashbacks and ghosts and episodes like 'Elliot's Wonderful Life' (10/11 by Tony McHale)."

So which shows currently influence Holby?

"If Tony was all about *The West Wing*, I'm all about *Grey's Anatomy*," says Simon.

"And I'm all about *Brothers and Sisters*," says Ollie.

Under showrunner Justin Young, Simon feels the show changed again. "Justin made it so grown up, somehow," he says. "He was the one who created the character of Hanssen and he had a great ambition of character and tone."

The current regime is proud of bringing a lot of humour to the show. "Ollie brought in this delicious twinkle," says Simon. "We hire people who get that sensibility, the twinkle and the humour."

STORY PRODUCER: KATE HALL

You have to give a writer room to care passionately and let go.
Everybody is raising the standard. – *Kate Hall*

On Holby, everything starts with character and story. And every story starts taking shape months—or even years before we see it on the screen, when the story team and the producers go to a hotel for a few days for their regular story conference.

They all assemble in a room, upwards of thirty people around a big table, where they thrash out ideas for upcoming stories. Once a year they look at long-term storylines, which will run over a year to three years. In between, quarterly meetings focus on the upcoming thirteen episodes.

Spearheading this process is story producer Kate Hall (who became series producer in 2017). She describes the long-term conference as a "blank piece of paper", and for her it's the most exciting part of the job. The writers pitch ideas to the room, talk around the table and/or get into smaller groups to brainstorm about particular characters. Several groups will consider the same character, and Kate says it's surprising how often there'll be a trend in the thinking.

Each character is considered in turn and there may be a specific issue that needs to be solved. For example, Kate had worked with Catherine

Russell previously and knew that Holby perhaps wasn't fully using her acting range, and especially her comic talents, when she first started on the show. The storyline about Serena's mother's dementia made the character more relatable and human, while her problems with her useless ex, Edward, also made people start to relate to Serena even more. The standalone episode where Ric and Serena went to Cambridge and we first discovered Serena's delightful relationship with Shiraz was a deliberate decision to place Serena with Ric, a character who was already a fan favourite. Kate says there's a "lot of strategic thinking involved".

A similar process happened with the character of Raf Di Lucca. His initial big story, the love triangle between him, his wife Amy and Dr Harry Tressler, wasn't bringing out all sides of Raf's character according to Kate. "Joe McFadden is very twinkly, so we had to show that natural warmth. Getting him and Serena drunk and giggling to bury Adrienne under a tree (17/7 'Flesh and Blood' by Jamie Crichton) was a good way to do that."

The story conferences come up with the big picture for the next series and a more solid picture of what the next thirteen episodes will look like, then the core writers and story team will focus on that thirteen-week block, deciding where the major beats of each story will fall. The stories will start to take shape, and an important consideration here is the overall tone of each episode. Kate is very mindful that Tuesday evening is not the time or place for doom and gloom. "It doesn't mean we can't tell difficult or edgy stories," she says, "But if we tell a story about a young man dying of cancer, he must have made his peace with that somehow, and any sudden death must have meaning or instruction for the family and friends left behind."

The pacing of the storylines is also important—are things playing out realistically and are fast-paced stories balanced by more slow-burning plots?

Kate feels her job as a story producer is to "ignite ideas" to encourage the writers to constantly come up with stories. She says Holby writers need to be able to speak their minds, but let go of an idea if it isn't working and listen to other people. "You have to give a writer room, to care passionately and let go," she says. "Writers are going to trump you. Everybody is raising the standard." She also feels a responsibility to the actors. "This is a character-led show," she says, "so good storylines allow these folks to do their best work, and I think character engagement is why Holby is successful."

Sometimes the actors are the starting point for a story idea. When Camilla Arfwedson joined to play Zosia, there hadn't been the intention of portraying Zosia as having a mental health issue, but writer Julia Gilbert suggested the storyline after Holby staff noticed that Camilla's performance had a vulnerability about it. They knew she'd be able to convincingly play the storyline and at the same time the existing back story made sense of this diagnosis.

"You're thinking, how can we push the actors into something we've never seen them do before?" says Kate, giving as another example the character of Dominic, and how the Dominic/Isaac story would bring out another aspect of David Ames's portrayal. "Dominic is a 'mask-wearing' character, as are various others on the show. You need to know what's behind the mask when you're writing stories and how much of it you're going to reveal at any point."

The characters aren't just considered as individuals, but also in terms of how they relate to the other people in their group. Compared to a lot of long-running shows, Holby doesn't have a large regular cast, so it's important that each character is able to generate stories within their group. It helps if a character can impact on more than one person. For example in series 17 Mo's father Clifford provided an interesting new aspect to Mo, but just as important was his interaction with Fletch.

As well as bringing new people in, killing them off can also lend further story opportunities. The death of Fletch's wife meant that a whole new set of stories was available to Fletch about his status as a single parent and his financial struggles. Fletch was too proud to ask for help and this led him down a criminal path with Clifford. As a result, Adele got hurt and Fletch's feelings of guilt led to him trying to atone for that by holding a live grenade and saving Guy Self's life in a memorable and dramatic episode (17/48 'An Eye for an Eye' by Nick Fisher).

Occasionally the well of story ideas for a particular ward seems to run a little dry, usually because so much has already been done with those characters. That's when characters might be moved to different parts of the hospital so they can interact with a different set of characters, or a new character might be brought in.

When the writers felt they needed a fresh angle for Jac Naylor, they brainstormed about everyone associated with her life. The idea of someone from her past life in care walking into her present came up and that's where the idea came about for the character of Fran Reynolds (Carli Norris). "I wanted something massive for Jac at Christmas, with Emma apparently at risk," (18/11 'Blue Christmas' by Julia Gilbert) Kate says. When Fran arrived she was already friends with Essie, "so there's shorthand and you can find out a lot about her quickly," says Kate. "Then there's layers we can start peeling away. We purposefully made sure we didn't cross her with Jac until she'd been established, then the minute she sets eyes on Jac you see a change in her demeanour and you're wondering what that's about, then you get a massive reveal. We all got really excited about that and thought, 'Let's get her on the roof!'"

At the same time, plans were being made to bring in the character of Jac's half-sister, Jasmine (Lucinda Dryzek). "They're brilliant on screen," Kate told me. "You can see the connection between the two of them and believe it." Fran would later be brought back when Lucinda Dryzek said she wanted to leave, to play out the storyline about Jasmine's death.

The writers are always thinking in terms of oppositions—positive and negative thinkers, extroverts and introverts. Kate says, "Opposition creates great story," and this was seen in the struggle between Guy Self and Henrik Hanssen for control of the hospital in series 17. "I always say if you were going to build a monument to Guy Self it would be a huge phallic symbol," says Kate. "He's apparently purely self-regarding. A monument to Hanssen would be a honeycomb because he sees the world in cooperative Swedish terms, where everybody is contributing."

Several people told me that the restrictions of having a relatively small regular cast mean that coming up with stories for Holby is actually more interesting, and Kate agrees. "I love it, because it's really tough to storyline," she says. "There aren't stunts and locations, there's only a handful of characters, but those restrictions are really exciting. The team here are lovely, the actors are phenomenal and I'm really proud of the work we do."

LINE PRODUCER: LYNN GRANT

Sometimes people can think, 'I've not heard from Lynn for a while,'
and that's because everything's going like clockwork. – *Lynn Grant*

The line producer's role is to look after the budget of the show in terms of having an overview about what the show needs and what is financially possible to deliver. For the past ten years, that's been the job of Lynn Grant, who first joined Holby as a production manager in 2001, the first year the show was on screen fifty-two weeks a year. It's a massive job. As well as the financial side, Lynn is also responsible for making sure Holby is legally compliant with the way BBC Studios require them to operate in terms of business processes, training, health and safety and data protection.

Lynn's favourite part of her job is that she's ultimately responsible for crewing the units who work on the show. "We obviously need the best people we can get who work on our sort of show and can do the show as quickly as we need to film," she says. "One of the biggest things I love is to find the next generation that's going to come in and see this as a step up."

Everyone on Holby is proud of the way the finished programme looks. "For the money it looks really sexy and it's lit really well, and I get a lot of DOPs (director of photography, the person responsible for

29

the overall photography and look of a film or television programme) asking what camera we use." The camera is an Amira, originally made for documentaries. Holby was one of the first dramas to use it. "There's lots of sides to the job that enable you to have creative interest in it," says Lynn. "It's not just about process and logistics."

On the day I talked to Lynn in May 2017 she'd been working on the budget for the rest of series 19, which was due to run for sixty-four episodes, instead of the usual fifty-two, for internal BBC reasons, so twelve extra weeks' budget had to be allocated. She told me it had to be done line by line into every single category that makes the show, "From salaries to design to makeup to prosthetics. That's very time consuming because you've got to put it in exactly to the penny what you need to make that number of episodes for each department. And the next thing is I've got to write memos to all those departments to say what their extra money is so they know what they're able to spend."

She was also starting to arrange a standalone episode that was due to start filming, including letting the medical advisers know the date of the medical meeting. Lynn starts to get the team together for the episode, before handing it off to a production manager.

Lynn is the person who has to keep a practical, financial eye on what the story team plans to do. For example, the writers might have written some scenes to take place in an outside location or a set which would need to be specially built. Lynn has to decide whether it would be financially and practically feasible, or whether they need to make changes to the script such as having the same story play out within the hospital. "That's when you get those funny devices with somebody's mother coming in as a patient, and then we can bring some other character in with them," she says. "We've got enough money to say yes to most things, as long as we're saying no to some things. It's a balance."

Sometimes the story will require an expensive episode. In 17/21 ('Trust In Me' by Jon Sen), Dr Harry Tressler fell from a window-cleaning platform. Lynn had to factor in that this sequence would take extra days to film (including a Sunday), so the crew would have to be booked for longer than usual, and there was a difficult stunt to arrange. There was the added complication of the special prosthetics required for

Jules Knight's face in the ensuing episodes, as we saw the outcome of his injuries. For a complex prosthetic, a member of the prosthetics team is required on set during filming, in case the prosthetic starts to move or peel away. This takes them away from their workshop making things for other episodes, so their time has to be factored in. "If that gets out of control and they feel it's all building up on them, they'll come to me and I'll have to find a way we can lose something from another episode to give them back that time," Lynn explains.

She emphasises that it's not about telling the editorial team what they can't do, but about finding ways for them to do as much as they can within the budget and keeping expectations realistic. "I think it's really not nice to have a writer sat at home thinking big about the stories and they come in just to be told 'can't afford that,'" she says. "That just leaves me with a horrible taste in my mouth. So I'm very keen to not get them set off on a road that's not going to lead to a script they'd like to tell."

When Lynn first joined Holby in the first fifty-two-episode year in 2001, there were two teams working at a time, blue and green. She was the production manager of the blue team and they filmed every single week without a break for a year. It wasn't a sustainable way of working in the long term, so they introduced a third team, so that each team had some downtime and preparation time. They worked out a pattern to make this work, and now they have teams X, Y and Z. On some days there will be three units filming at a time and this means that each team can have nine days of downtime before they start filming again.

Lynn's long history with the show has given her a lot of background knowledge. "I can be the spoilsport," she says, "because there aren't many stories we haven't covered." One of the things that keeps popping up in story ideas over the years involves the use of robots. "I always say, 'But it isn't a real robot, it's a prop robot,'" she says. "Anything that looks high-tech enough to be believable would cost thousands of pounds and that's where the budget runs out. We did have a real robot once. We were going to do this story about a real robot, and it wouldn't fit in the lift, so we just had to use the top half of it upstairs in Darwin, and the bottom half stayed downstairs! That's the only time we've seen a real one, otherwise they've been props. They're never going to let us use a real, very expensive robot on a prosthetic because you'll ruin what it's meant to do on a real body."

You might remember a storyline in Series 12 where Connie Beauchamp became director of robotics for a while. That robot was a prop. "Connie had the robot and Michael Spence broke it, so it was a funny story and we got away with it being a made one," Lynn says. "We had one once, and it had prop men behind it moving it, and the crew were laughing their heads off because they couldn't get it to do that smooth move that robots have. So even though in research we still hear that robotics is the future, it's a hard one to interpret on our budget, so I tell them to steer clear."

Lynn, like Kate Hall, finds creative possibilities in restrictions. She says, "Sometimes not being able to do something leads us somewhere that's more successful than the original idea. For example an artist we wanted turns out not to be available, and initially there's disappointment, but a new idea springs from it and the new idea might be loved. As you pursue the new idea you suddenly think 'Do you remember? We were only doing that because of that.' Continuing drama is always open and you just have to think 'What happens if…?' What happens if that actor decides to move on and we've just storylined for them? Because I've been here so long and worked with so many series producers, I know you can always change things and work around it."

The key thing for Lynn is to keep producing episodes of the quality that people have come to expect. "It was mooted about Holby having a live episode once," she says, but the idea wasn't considered for long. "It wasn't so much the actors. It was prosthetics. We didn't know how that could be done live. With Holby you get the best episode for the viewer when it's been through post-production and it's edited. The consensus was that editing allows for nice things to happen. If you did a live ep on this show it would be very limited."

PRODUCER: SARAH CREASEY

Every day is just fun for all sorts of reasons. – *Sarah Creasey*

Sarah Creasey is one of Holby's producers. This means she has day-to-day responsibility for blocks of two episodes as they go, so she's involved from when the writer is commissioned to produce the script. From commissioning she works closely with the script editor and the writer, developing the script. She then hires the director and works with her or him pre-shoot with casting of guests, sometimes sitting in on the casting, and sometimes just signing them off.

Sarah is on hand to answer any questions that the director or the casting department might have before the shoot, then when shooting is underway she'll be on set to make sure everything is okay. When the episodes have been shot, the producer will sit in on the edit with the director and the editor, before the episodes are finally sent to Kate Hall and Simon Harper for approval. "It's just essentially managing it all and making sure it all goes to plan," she says. "It's a varied job. It's a massive job, but it's so much fun, it's really great."

Like a lot of people at Holby, Sarah has had different roles there over the years. Her dad worked in TV, so it was always something that was in her life. "My first job was work experience here in the research room," she says. "I remember thinking I either wanted to be a runner or a researcher, having no idea how different those two jobs were at all. Then I realised I wanted to go down the editorial route. I've been producing for two years. Before that I script-edited on Holby, and I was senior script editor on *EastEnders*, so I worked my way up the editorial route. I've been a script researcher and a story researcher. It's good because it means I understand everyone's jobs really well."

Sarah says the toughest part of her job is getting the scripts absolutely right, and ready in time. "Every journey you go on with a script is different and varied and challenging. When you're most stressed is when you've got a script that you know can be brilliant, but you're running out of time."

As a producer Sarah has to help ensure that Holby has a consistent look and values. "I think we're all doing that all the time," she says, "And because I've worked on Holby in practically every job, it's just intrinsic to me now. I live and breathe Holby. Certainly if I'm bringing a new director on it's really important for them to understand the Holby style. There's a line. We want to make sure we're taking risks and doing new things and doing cool new stuff, so we are pushing the boundaries as much as possible—but at the same time what you don't want is to be using a shot that jars you out of watching it. You want the audience not really to notice, but we know that we're doing it. So if a director wants to try something unusual or risky, we try to make sure that they've shot it more conventionally as well, so if we think it isn't working in the edit we can just cut it. The worst is when they do a shot that doesn't quite work and they've got nothing else to go to. We've got lots of directors who are doing awesome stuff. It's looking really filmic at the moment I think. You've got to take those risks."

She mentioned episode 19/27 ('Someone to Look After Me' by Patrick Homes), which was the climax of the Dominic/Isaac storyline where Dominic fell down the hospital stairs. There was a scene where Dominic was on a trolley, slipping in and out of consciousness, and Hanssen and Zosia were talking to him. "It was all like a dream sequence," she says, "And Karl Neilson, the director, did it all on green screen on Keller. That's not the kind of thing we normally have time to do but we managed, and I think it looked amazing. It was a special episode and we wanted to make sure we had special stuff in it."

Karl Neilson also directed the episode that ended with Serena and Bernie on the roof in deck chairs (19/26 'It's Only Love If It Hurts' by Sarah Creasey and Nick Fisher). "Karl really preps," Sarah says. "He's so meticulous in making sure he knows before he goes on to set exactly what's going to happen. He's up nights doing it, making sure it looks amazing. And it's all worth it. He'll always have these bold ideas that just elevate the episode." Karl had a vision for the script that included the idea of us seeing Bernie, Jasmine and Fletch from the outside of the building as they ran up the stairs, and using a drone to film up and over and around the scene on the roof. "Serena being on the roof with her wine and cigarette and everything, that was all [writer] Nick Fisher," Sarah explains. "Karl was very clear that he wanted to put her in that red coat. I asked Catherine Russell [Serena] what music she thought Serena would be listening to when everything's falling apart, and she said 'Blondie!' So we put Blondie on there."

Sarah also revealed that the story of Serena bullying Jasmine was originally going to be Bernie bullying Jasmine. "We changed that when we found Catherine was going off on her break," she says. The original version of the Jasmine bullying story would have kicked off with the death of Bernie's daughter Charlotte, rather than Serena's daughter Elinor. The story would have played out almost identically, but it was swapped around neatly when Catherine said she wanted some months off. It was one of the occasions where outside circumstances forced a change in the storyline which made it turn out better than the story that had originally been planned. "In the end it was quite special," Sarah says.

I ask Sarah if there was anyone she'd like to see back at Holby. "Isaac," she says straight away. "It would be quite hard to reform his character though! Marc Elliott is so much fun and he was such a great character. I'd bring Arthur back if I could. I always think it would be fun to have Michael [Spence] from the old days. Hari Dhillon would be really awesome. Joseph [Byrne]. I used to love Sam Strachan and Joseph and that friendship. That Jac and Joseph quarantine episode [11/24 'Locked Away' by Graham Mitchell] was brilliant."

Like everyone on Holby, Sarah loves her job. "It's such a family and that, for me, is the most fun part of it. It's being surrounded by people you really get on with and really respect. Every day is just fun for all sorts of reasons. It's so rare for people to genuinely love their job. I never take it for granted."

SERIES PRODUCTION MANAGER: ALI LIDDLE

People say 'If no one knows, Ali will know,'
and I usually do. – *Ali Liddle*

"If you want to know anything about Holby, just ask Ali," I was told before I'd even met her. As a long-time fan of both *Holby City* and *Casualty*, Ali has an encyclopaedic knowledge of both shows and is the person everyone goes to if they want to check something. Ali has been working on Holby full time since July 2007 (Series 8, though she worked for a while on Series 7), and she's watched it since the very first episode. "I wouldn't say I remember everything as far back as day one," she says, "But I just generally retain a lot of information."

Ali typically starts work at 7am, and works until 7pm, but this can vary depending on the time of year. "If you're shooting in summer and you need it to be dark, it won't be dark by 7pm." She starts the day by checking that everyone has arrived and is okay. "The actors will be going through costume and makeup from 7am, so the team will be checking that everyone's here and nobody's stuck on a train, or had a breakdown in their car, or ill." Ali goes to set for the first line run and rehearsal of the day to check there aren't any last-minute problems, and then goes back to her desk in the large open-plan office on the fifth floor to start planning ahead for the next block of filming.

Cast members often come to the fifth floor to talk to the staff about anything that's concerning them. Ali makes a point of welcoming new people. "It can be quite daunting when people start on a show like this, especially if they haven't done anything like this before and they don't know how it works," she says. "I tell them if they don't know who to ring, they can call me." At the same time, she says it's a very friendly show and everyone is approachable.

Ali loves the variety of her job. "It's always different bits of busy," she says. We were talking in September 2016 and she'd just worked on 19/8 ('Parasite' by Simon Norman), the one where Matteo Rossini arrived on a horse. "So there was a lot to do with the horse!"

She also loves the friendliness of the place. "We get a lot of repeat crew," she says (all the Holby crew are freelance). "They like working here, it's like a big family." She says all the actors are lovely and she stays in touch with people after they've left. If she could bring anyone back, her first choices would be Elliot Hope and Michael Spence. "I also loved Jimmy Akingbola as Malick. I liked Don Gilet (Jesse Law), he's lovely. I still talk to Duncan Pow, who played Linden." Ali also mentions the supporting artists, some of whom have been with Holby for years.

Ali described how the production teams work. "There are fifty-two episodes a year and we shoot those in blocks of two. We do twenty-five blocks, which makes fifty episodes and means we can have two weeks off at Christmas. In order to get the two extra episodes, we do 'standalone' episodes, single episodes which usually take us out of the hospital. We do them twice a year and they can be filmed alongside the other blocks." You can usually recognise those episodes because they don't fit the usual Darwin, Keller, AAU three-story format. The standalone episode will usually only have two stories, one on location and one in the hospital. Examples of these would be 15/13 'Hanssen/Hemingway' by Justin Young (the episode set partly in Stockholm) and 19/13 'I Do, I Do, I Do' by Michelle Lipton (Mr T and Inga's wedding). Episode 13 of the series is often a standalone, as it falls just after New Year.

"We have three teams who do the eps," Ali says. "Each team will be working on a different block, and all will be at different stages in the production process." When I talked to Ali in September 2016, her team was just about to start shooting on episodes 14 and 15 of series 19, which would be transmitted in January 2017. "The team next to me are finishing 9 and 10, and the team beyond that are doing 11 and 12," Ali said. "It takes twenty days to shoot a block of two episodes. We've got one block starting today, one's in its third week and one's just finishing its last couple of days. So we've got three units working today, one unit on Darwin, one on Keller and one on AAU. Today my team are doing a whole day in Darwin from episode 14."

For the actors, this means that often they shoot scenes out of sequence. In the storyline where Fletch was stabbed (18/47 'Protect and Serve' by Joe Ainsworth), the actual stabbing was shot after the episodes that were seen afterwards, where the effects of the stabbing and his paralysis were shown, because the stabbing was in the standalone episode which was shot out of order with the others. "The actors might have three or four scripts in their head at any one time," Ali says, "So it's quite a discipline for them to remember, 'Do I know that yet? Have I found that out yet?', and all that kind of thing."

Ali explained that Holby is shot with a single camera. This gives the show a much more filmic look, but it takes more time to film.

"Something like *EastEnders* is multi-camera. It's shot with a vision mixer in the gallery, so it's being cut as it goes along. Holby and *Casualty* are like a lot of dramas and films, we shoot single camera. So you and I will be talking on a sofa scene, and they'll do what they call a master shot from over there of the two of us sitting chatting. Then they might put the camera on me, and we do the scene again with you feeding me the lines, then they move the camera to be looking at you and we do the scene again with me feeding you the lines. So they've got to light every take separately. For the actors it means they have to replicate their performances and also what they did in those performances. So not only have they got to say the lines the same, but if somebody picks up the phone or something, they have to do it exactly the same in every take, otherwise it would be impossible to edit seamlessly. This is the technical side of acting, and it's something that somebody like Alex Walkinshaw (Fletch) is very good at."

"While this is happening the script supervisor will be marking down how long the shots are, and watching the continuity. It's quite a skill to be able to watch what someone's doing, watch the script at the same time, watch their continuity of action, checking their eye-lines."

There are a lot of people involved in the production crew, as Ali explains. "The assistant directors (ADs) get all the people through costume and makeup. Calls for costume and makeup start at 7am. If people have to have injuries, they go through prosthetics and all that's got to be worked out in the order of shooting scenes as well to get people on set for an 8am start. Each team has their own coordinator, then on the floor we have the first AD, who works to the director. They run the floor and take over the schedule from the schedulers and tailor the fine scheduling of the block and work out what to do. The second AD, who is their right hand person in the office, does the daily call sheet based on the information we've got from the schedule of what time they want people on set, and any additional crew and equipment that might be needed. They'll check the call sheet and wait downstairs in the morning with the third AD who works on set with the first AD and directs all the supporting artists, and the floor runner who works to get them on the floor and gets the radios out, checks if anyone wants a drink and cues people. Runners are the most junior of the AD team on the floor, but also a vital part of it."

When an episode has been shooting for a couple of days, it goes to the editing department so they can begin the process of putting the final episode together. "So as well as looking at the eps we're doing today and going down for the line runs on the floor and going through any queries by the cast, the producer has also been in editing looking at the first cut-together episode and giving her notes of the previous block that's finished editing," Ali says. "Meanwhile the people in editorial are working on future stories and scripts. You have to have a lot in your head!"

SCHEDULING: LORNA WHITTAKER

We have to know which story is going to be shooting
where and with whom. – *Lorna Whittaker*

The logistics of getting fifty-two episodes of Holby filmed in fifty weeks, and employing two or three film crews, multiple sets and all of the actors and guests as efficiently as possible, seems like a brain-bending task. This is the job of series scheduler Fiona Naylor and scheduler Lorna Whittaker.

Lorna explains what is involved. "There's always two teams filming, so we have to make sure that both teams can always be shooting with our small core of artists and the guests that come in," she says. "We shoot in pairs of episodes, so I schedule a pair of episodes and we do alternate pairs. We use a software package called Movie Magic. It's the industry standard, that everybody schedules on. We physically put the scripts into the computer, with the story plan that we've worked out with the story department, and we work out where everybody's going to film on which day to get the episodes done in the twenty days that we shoot."

Lorna schedules ten weeks ahead, while Fiona works with the story team to plan even further ahead than that, between three and six months. The longer-term plans aren't done with computer software and are more general, but it's important to know at an early stage that it's going to be physically possible to film the scripts in the given time. "Otherwise we'd all be playing on the same ward with the same people," Lorna explains. "Obviously artists are entitled to holidays, so we have to work round that, and they can have hospital and doctors appointments we have to work round. We've got time to change things if we're aware of problems that may arise, but we work with the story department to change things. So if an artist comes in and asks for some leave, we liaise with the story team to see how we can make that work and that might mean a change of something in the script or a slight tweak to the schedule."

Even the best laid plans can sometimes go wrong, and tricky moments might come up if the writer makes changes to the story that haven't been planned—such as setting a scene in another location or using different characters. "If they want to do something different to what we've originally planned, that can have a knock-on effect for the stories working around it," Lorna says. "Further down the line, if they've already started filming and actors go off ill, things like that, we might have to change the schedules round and that can affect schedules we've still got in here, depending how long-term they are, or what they've had to bring forward in order to carry on filming."

When a script comes in, Lorna will put it into the Movie Magic software and will spend the day working out the schedule for the script. If she flags up anything that's going to be difficult to schedule, she feeds back notes to the story team, script editor and producer, letting them know that certain scenes may have to be cut or adjusted to fit the schedule. If she spots anything in the script that may cost extra money, that's also something that needs to be passed on. "They rely on us to alert them if there are too many stunts, for example, or a lot of stuff involving a child, or too much spread for the actors. Anything that might make the schedule difficult or unachievable we feed back on each draft to the script editor and the producer."

Potential problem areas can be spotted early. "We work very closely with the story team and will go to story conference, just to listen and see how the story might be moving on as an arc. We might spot potential problems that need to be ironed out before things get too far advanced," Lorna says. "Things like, if you have a bromance and the two characters are on different wards. It would mean they'd often want to cross them, and that's quite difficult sometimes and has to be planned and thought about. We don't have a big pool of artists, we only have sixteen regulars, which isn't a lot. It's not a lot to share between two or three teams." As Ali Liddle pointed out to me, "You couldn't have a story where the entire regular cast went out on a team-bonding exercise to the woods, because what would the unit back here get to do?"

Another thing that has to be planned around is the two standalone episodes, which are filmed as extras each year to bank enough episodes so that the entire production can shut down for two weeks at Christmas to give the staff a well-deserved break. "We do two stand-alones a year," Lorna says. "Usually half the story will be set on location and the other half will be set back here, so we just plan that episode early enough so we know which half of the story is going to be the location half. We block-book those days and we know who the main people are going to be in those stories, so we're shooting around that and we know we can't have those people filming back at Holby on those days."

Sometimes there are crossovers between *Holby City* and *Casualty*, and this presents another problem for the schedulers, and requires the scheduling teams of both shows to liaise. "The reason why there's not so many crossovers is because they film in Cardiff and we film in Elstree, and it's quite a long way away," Lorna says. "It's at least a day's travel— half a day to get here and half a day to get back—and we have to allow for that in the schedule. If the story team knows well enough in advance, we can liaise with their schedulers and make sure the people they may want, or we may want, aren't put into stories shooting at the same time. And the stories of both shows have to work—a character can't just be plopped in, their arc has to carry over so it has to be relevant. Also we're not filming the same episodes at the same time. *Casualty* film more ahead of us, so it's not like we're both filming episodes that are going to transmit in the same week. And they stop for two weeks in the summer and we don't, we only stop at Christmas." The main issue is geography. "Even if it was the same site, it would be something you'd have to plan for. You could go and grab someone for a couple of hours in an afternoon, perhaps, but as it is now, for one of our actors to do three scenes at *Casualty* requires at least two days of them being unavailable at Holby."

SCRIPT EDITOR: MATT DENISON

I think everyone who works here is a fan of the show. – *Matt Denison*

The script editor's job starts when she or he gets a storyline, which is a document detailing the three-story strands for the episode. There is a commissioning meeting with the writer, script editor, producer, series producer, story department, researcher and scheduler. They talk about the writer's response to the story and initial ideas, and the writer will pitch ideas for guest storylines. The meeting will discuss whether the guest story might be too similar to something that's recently been seen, or whether it's appropriate for the 8pm time slot and the general tone of *Holby City*. Then the writer will go away and produce a first draft.

"I see it as my job not to get too heavily detailed in the first draft stage," script editor Matt Denison says. "I think in the first two drafts you get structure and tone correct. In the third draft you start doing the finer points of character and dialogue and making those lines really sing. There'll always be a line in a script that could be better and pushed a little further." He's very mindful of not stifling the creative process with too much criticism, though. "You have to help the writer keep the joy of the script," he says. "They're personally invested in the story and have spent weeks on it. It's not about wrapping the writers in cotton wool, but it is about maintaining the excitement and the love of writing."

The script editor will also filter in notes from the director, producer and executive producer, and make sure the script is progressing through the various drafts so it comes in on time. The script producer, Sophia Rashid, has oversight of all episodes in the series and keeps a view of continuity from one episode to the next and across the series. She allocates scripts to particular writers, and all scripts are scheduled with when each draft is expected to come through. The script editor has to keep on top of this timetable. If the writer should fall behind at any stage, the time will have to be made up elsewhere. "The one date you can never shift is the day you start shooting," says Matt.

Matt says Holby is a difficult show to write for. "We're a sister show to *Casualty*, but the difference between Holby and *Casualty* is vast. We don't tend to invest in the guest characters' lives as much as they do in *Casualty*, but we have more of an investment in our serial elements and our regular characters' lives and we follow them on their journeys in a personal and in-depth way. From a tonal point of view we have what Simon (Harper) refers to as 'the Holby twinkle', the sparkle element which is that fine balance between comedy and drama. We have a sense of humour and a joy and a camaraderie, because that's what keeps people tuning in, I think."

One episode he's particularly proud of working on was 19/14 'Aces High' by Joe Ainsworth, who has been writing for Holby since 2004. This was the episode where Dominic Copeland's parents, Carole and Barry, came back to the hospital when Dominic was still trying to keep his relationship with Isaac quiet. Matt says the original idea was that Carole was going to be ill and that's how she would find out about Isaac.

"Joe really wanted to bring Barry back in because there was a lot of unresolved story from the seaside episode [17/50 'At First I Was Afraid' by Julia Gilbert] and Barry's rampant homophobia and disdain for his son. We wanted to show that he was changing, growing, getting better, and we wanted to show that Carole hadn't been a mug for staying with her husband," Matt says. "I loved that story because we showed lots of sensitivity in the thawing of the relationship between Dom and his father, and then you bring in Isaac. At the time we didn't fully know how dangerous he was, it was a very slow-burning story. The bit I adored was that bit at the end where he's very subtly dismissive of Carole and she realises that this man is a danger to her boy, but she doesn't try to mollycoddle Dom in any way, she just tells him to take care of himself and leaves it in his hands. Joe did such a wonderful job of that family unit, it was really nuanced and lovely. So I was particularly proud of that and its place in the broader arc of Dom and Isaac which has just been one of our best storylines, because it was so long and slow-burning."

Matt had a lot of praise for the medical research team in general, but specifically for the work they'd done on the domestic abuse storyline. "They were talking a lot to domestic abuse charities and they really wanted to get into the reality of what Dom would be feeling and how conflicted he would feel."

Holby is always aware of treating difficult subjects like alcoholism, depression or domestic abuse in a serious way. "You want to make sure you're doing it for a good reason, which is to raise awareness. I'm really proud when we can do those stories in a carefully paced way," Matt says, and admits he was shocked when he saw on Twitter the reaction of some of the audience to the Dominic and Isaac storyline. "So many fans were saying, 'Oh, kick him into touch', and I was thinking, it's not that simple. The story we're trying to tell is he really thinks Isaac loves him and cares about him. He's so emotionally vulnerable and has such low self esteem, which we've seeded all the way along. He's created this whole persona that isn't who he really is. It was all very consistent and I think we managed to tell that story really cleverly and I hope the message gets through to as many people as possible that you might not even realise you're in an abusive relationship until it's too late. Hopefully some of those people will be able to call those charities or get in touch and extricate themselves from horrendous situations like that."

Matt is constantly surprised and impressed with what the writers come up with. "I worked with Ed Sellek on episode 19/30 ['Gold Star']. It was jam-packed with little moments. I gave him a note saying, 'We need to have Hanssen vanish from the ward because he's hiding from Mr T's mother, but it would be great if he could be giving some pearls of wisdom to Oliver Valentine.'" Ed came up with a little scene where Hanssen and

Oliver Valentine were trying to get a chocolate bar that was stuck in the vending machine, and Fletch came along and got it unstuck. "I'd never in my wildest dreams have come up with a brilliant idea like that," Matt said. "Just the weird stiff-upper-lipness of Oliver and Hanssen." In the same episode we discovered that Hanssen was learning to play the theremin. "That worked on so many levels. It was a stroke of genius, and I was over the moon when I saw that in the script."

I was interested to know whether the actors got very involved discussing what their character would or wouldn't do or say. Matt said that his own role was generally over by the time the script reached the shooting stage, but if a producer was away and an actor had a query, the script editor might need to go to set if the director wanted anything about the script explaining. "I remember in 19/30 ['Gold Star' by Ed Sellek] Ric orders a round of shots and says, 'Do you think you can hack it, Oliver?' and Oliver says, 'I was in Juarez, we drank mescal like it was…' and the original line was 'soy lattes'. And James (Anderson) said, 'But you can't drink soy lattes fast, you have to sip them because they're really hot.' So the line became apple juice or orange juice or something. Small little line tweaks like that you can allow. Anything that is larger you have to give the writer the opportunity to respond, but the pace here is so relentless sometimes we just have to make those decisions on the fly."

Matt thinks that everyone who works on Holby is a fan of the show and he's watched it himself since the beginning, dipping in and out over the years depending on what was going on in his life. So he did have some gaps in his knowledge when he started working there. "I was never around for Guy Self's introduction and I found understanding his character and Zosia's relationship to him quite alien to me, so I had to ask for a lot of help," he says. He'll often ask his colleague, producer Irma Inniss, who has an 'encyclopaedic' knowledge of recent Holby history. "Generally I was asking a lot more questions at first and now I have it all up here, I hope. It's more about an understanding of the deeper characterisation and the tone of the show. It's about knowing what the characters would say and do."

SCRIPTWRITERS: ANDY BAYLISS, NICK FISHER AND PATRICK HOMES

It's a messy, annoying, hair pulling, head
banging, wonderful thing! – *Nick Fisher*

Andy Bayliss is the lead writer on *Holby City* and among his writing credits is the episode where Arthur Digby died (18/35 'I'll Walk You Home'). He came from storylining and script editing on various shows, "until I finally got the courage to do a trial script for *Casualty*, and from there, Holby."

Nick Fisher was approached to write for Holby by Simon Harper, after he saw a series called *Manchild* that Nick had created, as well as episodes of *Hustle* and *New Tricks* that he'd written. "At the time he felt my lighter, more fun and warm character writing would suit the show," Nick says.

Patrick Homes was a storyliner and script editor on *Family Affairs* and *The Bill*. He was a full-time writer for *The Bill* and when that ended he applied for a place on the BBC Writers Academy. Just as he was about to start that, a writer on Holby pulled out of doing a script and the producer, who knew Patrick from his work on *Family Affairs*, rang to ask if he could step in.

"Holby scripts walk a tightrope of drama and comedy and medicine," according to Nick. "It's a very complicated mix. Other soaps just have drama—maybe a bit of farming thrown in. Holby is religious in its inclusion of medicine—real, properly researched medicine—and surgery specifically. This makes the scripts very complicated things to write and to be fair it does eat up a lot of writers along the way. I have written for many other shows and I can safely say that nothing is as hard work as Holby. It might not look it on screen sometimes, but the construction of these episodes is sometimes gruelling. At the same time I have learned more about writing on Holby than on any other show I've ever worked for or invented."

"*Holby City* never stops," Patrick Homes says. "It's fifty-two weeks a year. So story generation is a constant ongoing process. Because it's constant, stories have to be fluid as well to a certain extent. Actors may leave. Things might not work quite as you thought, real-life events may dictate a change in the story." Rarely, the course of a character's time in the show might be decided right from the start. "One time a story was set in stone was when we introduced Tara Lo in series 14. At that story conference we made a commitment for her to die from her brain tumour after eighteen months or so. This is sometimes helpful because it keeps you focused on the outcome and you don't get distracted into side stories."

Patrick finds inspiration in real life and current issues in the NHS. "For big, long-running arcs, it's sometimes helpful to base them on epic stories in culture. Shakespeare obviously is always a good start for any story. I've always wanted to do a story about Hanssen and his son Fredrik based on *Le Morte D'Arthur*—the source for the film *Excalibur*—with Hanssen as King Arthur, Fredrik as Mordred and Holby City as Camelot!"

Nick's inspiration comes from, "Everywhere. Life. The doctor's surgery, the harbour, the paper, the radio, my wife, my children, the men at my local garage, Kevin my dairy farmer neighbour, the badminton club, my dodgy past, my dad's old folks home—everywhere." Real-life events are often used as a springboard for the writers' ideas ("it would be silly not to try and encompass some of the real-life hospital world," Nick Fisher says), but events would be tweaked and changed to fit in with the characters and the show, and to avoid any legal or moral difficulties in the real world.

Andy Bayliss says he enjoys writing for all the characters equally. Nick Fisher agrees to a certain extent. "They're all good to write for. To be honest it's the story and who they're interacting with that makes it exciting. A good story and good chemistry with the other characters in the scene are what makes it a joy to write." He does admit to finding Elliot Hope "a treat" to write for, and he enjoys writing for Dominic and Sacha. Patrick Homes says it tends to change as he writes different episodes. "Jac is very easy to write for because she's such a defined character, but I think Serena has been the most fun and provided the most range in my time. And Arthur Digby was a joy to write."

Holby is, of course, first and foremost a medical drama. Andy Bayliss explains how the medical details are incorporated into the story. "Holby has a research department who work with some amazing medical advisers, who are actual doctors, nurses, surgeons etcetera. It's up to the writer to work out how they want to tell the guest story, what beats they need to hit, or the shape of it, if you like, and then they pass it over to the folks who know what they're talking about medically to provide possible scenarios. It's then a back and forth between the three parties to find a compromise in terms of what could realistically happen and what gives the most intrigue and drama."

This means inevitably that concessions have to be made. Viewers occasionally grumble that a patient recovers from heart surgery remarkably quickly on Holby, but it's a drama and the story has to be told within the hour. "Sometimes things are truncated, because we can't take six weeks for someone to get better," production manager Ali Liddle says. "It's okay if it's a regular character and you can see some kind of progress or story, how they battle back, like Fletch after being stabbed in series 18, but you have to engage an audience and you don't want to give them a reason to go off and make a cup of tea. The patients are there to help the story, not hinder."

Audience reaction to a particular storyline usually comes too late to influence the story at the beginning. "We're writing six months ahead," Nick Fisher says. "So by the time the story is on screen there will be more of it already written. If it's not going down well and still being told, then there's a chance we would begin to modify it or else drop it out of focus. There's a lot of audience monitoring going on which does get fed back to the team. These days with Twitter and online reviewing there's a lot of reaction out there. Often executives or series producers will feed this into story conference and that might affect further decisions."

Patrick Homes says he reads online forums to check how characters and stories are being received. "You do tend to check if the audience believes in a particular long-term relationship," he says. "If they don't, then you have a problem."

Nick doesn't read anything about the show online, and feels that, "The best stories are always the ones which we work hard on getting right in the first place and then hold our nerve and see them through to the end, like the death of Arthur."

Anyone spending any time on an online Holby forum will fairly soon come up against the complaint that no romantic couples are allowed to be happy for long. Patrick says that the simple answer is conflict. "Conflict is drama. Conflict generates story. Stability and happiness do not. Stability and happiness are the reward of overcoming conflict. As soon as you achieve stability and happiness you lose conflict and, therefore, story." He says it's as frustrating for the writers as it is for the audience. "We often sit down and swear that this relationship will be stable and happy and reflect the vast majority of relationships in life. And then we get into the story room and... blank."

Asked about favourite episodes, Nick Fisher said he couldn't remember them all but was proud of some of the guest characters he'd written, and it is a colourful list: "The ice cream van, the hand grenade man, the young farmers, the orange-faced armoured car robber, the whelk fisherman, the sea-shanty-singing group of crab potters..."

Patrick Homes says 19/17 ('Of Lions and Lambs') was a particular favourite among his recent episodes. "It came together in its directing, performances and 'feel' just perfectly. It was a difficult story, with grief and anger for Serena and the destruction and abuse of Dominic's character and self-worth by Isaac. Catherine Russell and David Ames played blinders and the director, Karl Neilson, gave it a slightly heightened feel that was just great." He feels the whole Dominic/Isaac story was "a difficult story, told well over a long period."

Andy Bayliss thinks the thing that sets Holby apart even from its sister show *Casualty* is the tone. "*Casualty* is much more plot-driven, with big guest stories, the accident and so on. Holby, by its nature, has to be character-led. But humour goes a long way in both, I think. Humour and heart."

MEDICAL RESEARCHERS: HAYLEY CAMERON, KEREN COLEMAN, HANNAH GORAYA AND LINA STROUD

You can walk in on us on the phone and we'll be saying, 'Up the bum? Or down the mouth? And what colour is the fungus?' – Lina Stroud

I used to wonder how *Holby City*'s writers were so clued-up on medical things. How did they come up with so many exotic mystery illnesses that would have even the finest fictional doctors in the land scratching their heads and resorting to Holby's fictional version of Google, Whippet Search? How did they make three ailments a week neatly fit the story they wanted to tell?

The answer is that every Holby script is a team effort, and on the medical side that includes medical researchers, plus advisers who are actual doctors and experts in their field.

The medical research team have their own large office on the fifth floor at Holby HQ. I spoke to Hayley Cameron, Lina Stroud, Hannah Goraya and Keren Coleman about what they do.

Hayley told me that the first thing that happens is that the writer of a particular episode will send them a scene-by-scene breakdown, which is the basic storyline with added comments such as, "It would be really good if the patient could have a crisis here," or, "I really want a condition that makes the patient look bad so they're really insecure about their appearance." The research team pick all those things out and then get on the phone to one of the medical advisers.

There are three core advisers—two general surgeons and one CT surgeon, plus a massive roster of people with different specialities, such as renal surgery and obstetrics. In addition, all of the transplant storylines are signed off by NHS Blood and Transplant.

The adviser will make suggestions about medical situations and conditions that would fit what the writer needs, and the researcher will then write up what they call a 'med journey' for the script, with the medical details that the writer needs.

Sometimes the writer will have come across a particular condition and will ask if that can be part of the story. Sometimes it isn't feasible and the researchers will pitch an alternative to them that will still work to tease out what they want from the characters. The essential point is that it needs to be medically accurate, but also that it needs to fit in with what can be achieved within the story.

"The more you learn, the more you explore, the more quickly you can respond when you're sitting in a meeting and the writer says they need a particular set of circumstances," Lina says. "You might remember something one of the medical advisers was talking about a while back that you couldn't use at the time, and it fits really well. It's fun when that happens."

After the writer has worked on the script for a while, a draft is sent back to the researchers who will send relevant parts of it to the relevant expert. So if a character has a baby, that part goes off to their obstetrics expert for feedback, which then gets put in a Word document and sent back to the writer. Some feedback forms will be very straightforward and just be a case of changing a word or two here and there. At other times it might be necessary to make big changes—for example, the order of medications might be wrong, or the writer might be portraying a particular condition as more (or less) serious than it would be in real life.

The CT adviser, Mr Shyam Kolvekar, has worked with *Holby City* since it started and knows exactly what the writers want. His attitude is, "Tell me what you want dramatically and I'll make it work." Lina says this will often be that they need more jeopardy: "I need blood to spurt on the walls. I don't care what it is, I just need a gusher!"

The next part of the process for the research team is doing a glossary for the script, breaking down the medical jargon phonetically for the actors and giving a basic description of what the terms mean, so the actors understand what they're saying.

Lina says that, more than any other drama she's heard of, the research team on Holby has to work really closely with the producers, story team and script editors. They all have to ensure that not only does the script stay medically accurate, it also has to represent the NHS in a thoughtful, respectful and realistic way, at the same time as facilitating the drama. "It's a very close-knit process," she says. "We might all be in different rooms, but we're all talking to each other all the time."

After a script for a particular episode has gone through three or four drafts, the director and assistant directors will sit down with the researchers, the makeup team and the prosthetics team to start to visualise the script in terms of how a particular condition would look —would the patient need a wheelchair? What prosthetics or makeup would be needed to make it look realistic? They need to be able to understand how to make it feasible that a patient with that condition would be looked after on one of Holby's regular wards and how to make it work in practice.

It was obvious to me how much all of the team loved the work they were doing. In fact it seemed to be so much fun that I was quite reluctant to leave them to it.

Lina says Holby is the nicest place she's ever worked in, and Hannah says, "If you care at all about drama it's a great place to learn. To find fifty-two new stories for each of those wards every year—it's just mind-boggling that you can do that in a way that still makes people tune in every single week. It's an amazing opportunity to be here and work at how they do that. This job is amazing."

CASTING: LIZ STOLL AND JOHN CANNON

Whenever you say you're a casting director, the first
thing people say is, 'Give us a job'. – *Liz Stoll*

Liz Stoll and John Cannon are responsible for casting the regular *Holby City* actors and also the guest artists. Liz is responsible for casting the speaking guests in a block of two episodes and John will cast the next block, working alternately.

The process starts when they get the scripts for the block and start making decisions about the people they'll need. They then put a breakdown on *Spotlight*, the UK's premier information service for actors. The breakdown will be a brief summary of what they're looking for and it goes out to about 260 agencies, who then send in suggestions for people who might be suitable for the roles.

The director then sits down with Liz or John to talk about her or his vision of how the character should be, and casting sessions will be set up. Four or five people will be seen, and with luck one of those will be suitable. If not, they keep going until they find the right person.

A practical consideration is that anyone who has appeared in either *Holby City* or *Casualty* previously can't be used as a different character within eighteen months, so they have a database to check this before someone is even approached.

Most guest artists will probably film for four or five days to cover their scenes, so it's important to check they'll be available on the days they're needed. Christmas, summer and bank holidays are always especially difficult, and John says, "You can guarantee the only days they aren't free are the days we need them. It happens so many times." Sometimes it's possible to rearrange the schedule to fit the availability of someone who's particularly wanted.

Potential guests are emailed the parts of the script that will be relevant to their character—both their actual lines and anything relating to them, such as conversations the doctors might have about their case. The director and casting director will choose three or so scenes for the candidates to read, and they will sometimes be asked to read a scene more than once to check how well they take direction. When the director and casting director have decided who they want, the name is sent to the producer, as well as the name of a back-up choice should the first choice become unavailable. The producer will either agree with the choice, or request the casting director to keep looking.

If they're casting for a regular cast member, Liz and John might receive over 500 suggestions from agents of people interested in the part, because "everyone wants to be a new regular on Holby". Normally twenty to thirty people will be seen and Liz and John will send the readings of the ones they think are most suitable to Kate Hall and Simon Harper. Out of those, they'll ask to see three or four. Usually they will be asked to do a screen test on a set. As they will usually be playing a doctor or a nurse, it's important that they can look convincing acting a medical procedure at the same time as speaking. This is particularly true for people with little previous TV experience.

Sometimes it might be essential that someone is found who has particular chemistry with an existing character. Rosie Marcel (Jac Naylor) was involved in Lucinda Dryzek's (Jasmine Burrows) screen test, because it was important that the two of them were believable as sisters. Other actors may have such extensive TV experience or profile that it's more a case of discussing the role with them to see if they're happy with it. Jemma

Redgrave (Bernie Wolfe) was asked whether she would be comfortable playing a gay character, and of course she said yes.

There are a number of assistants working in the casting department, and one of their jobs is to cast the child actors who sometimes appear. Children under the age of sixteen are only allowed to work a certain number of hours a day by law, so it's easier when casting for a fourteen-year-old character if they can be played by a sixteen year old. This isn't always possible, however.

Over the years there have been some high-profile guest artists in Holby, such as Maureen Lipman, Paul O'Grady, Keith Barron, Eric Sykes and Anita Dobson. Liz says the main lure for well-known actors is to be offered an interesting part. As it's known to be a nice show to work on, a lot of people are happy to be involved. John says, "We're lucky in that we've got a strong team, and it's rare to have location work, so they come in and everything runs really smoothly. It's a friendly unit and they know they're going to enjoy the work on a personal level as well as an artistic level."

Liz told me that a high-profile person she'd been really happy to get for three episodes (she didn't name names) said that it was one of the best jobs he'd ever done.

Liz and John have to be realistic about who they approach. As John points out, the series has its own reality and they wouldn't want the audience to spend the whole hour thinking, "Blimey, that's Michael Caine!" It would also be a complete waste of time to approach someone with the profile of Michael Caine. On the other hand, someone like Paul O'Grady was happy to take the role of Chrissie Williams's patient and friend Tim Connor in Series 15 because he thought it was a really nice story. The problem with Paul was that he was so busy with other commitments. "He's the busiest man in showbiz," says John. "He had his radio show, his dog show. We were having to courier him away on the back of a motorbike to his next thing. But as soon as we asked him he was really up for it."

While Michael Fassbender and Kate Winslet have both appeared in Holby, it was right at the beginning of their careers. "It's nice to find people on their way up," Liz says, "Or sometimes someone who has had a great career but hasn't worked for a while, for whatever reason."

It's part of the casting directors' remit to bring in as much diversity in the casting as possible and they are proud of the success they've had with this. Unless it's necessary because of a family connection, ethnicity wouldn't be specified in the script and so Liz says they aim to "throw the net as wide as possible. The most important thing is they're believable as a lawyer or dustbin man or whatever the part is".

For the character of Serena's nephew, Jason Haynes, they only saw actors who had a learning disability, because they knew Jason would have a learning disability himself. They chose Jules Robertson, who has Asperger's. Holby is trying to increase opportunities for actors with disabilities whenever possible.

As well as the time spent at Elstree (where they also do casting for other BBC shows such as *The Coroner* and *Father Brown*), Liz and John go to the theatre and cinema a lot to increase their knowledge of the actors around. They're both members of BAFTA, which involves watching a lot of films ready for the voting in January.

They often get invited to drama school showcases and John says he may be reading a script or looking at *Spotlight* and he'll remember someone he's seen in a drama school production who might be right for a part.

Sometimes a non-British person might be required. Liz went to Sweden to cast people for the series 15 episode partly set in Stockholm (15/13 'Hanssen/Hemingway' by Justin Young) and cast Pia Halvorsen as Hanssen's former partner. It often happens that the actors who are needed are based in London anyway, as was the case with Kaisa Hammarlund, who played Mr T's Swedish fiancée Inga. Liz already knew her from theatre productions.

When it came to casting Matteo Rossini, Liz and John contacted a lot of agents in Europe because they knew they were looking for someone non-British. Simon Harper had pitched the character at a story conference because he wanted to reflect the reality of the NHS by having a staff member who wasn't originally from the UK. The character was provisionally known as Xavier Cotillard, after the actress Marion Cotillard—Simon grew up in France and originally envisaged the character would be French.

They received tapes from France, Germany, Switzerland, Austria and Italy. Christian Vit, who was cast in the role, actually lived in England already. In Matteo's first episode we saw him riding a horse. John and Liz weren't told to only look at actors who could ride a horse, though. "They'd have found a way around it," Liz says. "Ultimately you're casting the actor as opposed to the skills." Luckily, Christian Vit had horse riding on his CV, and he'd honed his riding skills playing a Dornish guard in *Game of Thrones*.

A lot of people want to know how they can get a part in Holby. John's answer is simple: "You have to be an actor first."

"Everyone thinks they're an undiscovered star," says Liz. "There may be some brilliant undiscovered people out there, but there are only a certain number of parts and we can only see a certain number of people. How to get in is, work on your acting skills." The reality of working on a continuing drama is that the actors need to know what's required of them and have a certain amount of technique and expertise already.

I asked Liz if there was anyone she was particularly proud of discovering, and she said it would be a very rare instance where she would have been the first person ever to have seen someone's work, so she can't claim credit. She does, however, find it very satisfying to give someone their first job on Holby. "They tend to have done something we've seen before they come in. It's not some random person off the street." She'd first seen Lucinda Dryzek as a child actor when she was about ten years old and she was ideal when the part of Jasmine Burrows came up. Other people can seem very promising when Liz and John see them in school or university plays, but their skills don't translate to the audition room with a camera pointing at them.

Ellie Fanyinka (Morven Digby) described her audition. "I read it with John and Liz. They're very good actors! They do it enough – my goodness, they cast everything. They really helped me, they gave me lots of good tips. In the third audition they invite you to the studio and you do it in costume and you have to do a walk and talk so you have to be on set and put gloves on and stuff while you're saying the lines. So I did that with John, and Nigel Douglas was my director because they get a little hand-held camera and they get a director in to direct you. That was meant to be my final audition but they had to call me back again. So I had four auditions. Most people have three, and some people only have two. They said, 'We just need to see you one more time because we know you can do the kooky bit, but we're not sure if we believe she's a doctor.'" She laughs. "So they got me back for the fourth audition and I had to be a bit more serious and professional when I said, 'I think this is viral encephalitis.' In fact that was one of my lines!"

DIRECTOR: PAULETTE RANDALL MBE

I have a great time working here. But the *blood*... – *Paulette Randall*

Holby has many excellent directors and they each have their own way of working. I spoke to Paulette Randall because she directed the two episodes leading to Arthur Digby's death (18/34 'The Sky is Falling' and 18/35 'I'll Walk You Home,' both by Andy Bayliss), and I knew I wanted to do a chapter about that. I was amazed to discover that they were the first episodes she'd ever directed for Holby—or for television at all. She's hardly a newcomer, though. She was the associate director of the incredible 2012 London Olympics Opening Ceremony, has an extensive background directing in theatre, and was awarded an MBE in 2015 for services to drama.

Plus, everyone at Holby raves about her. Bob Barrett (Sacha Levy) says, "She's amazing. Sometimes she finishes the day early and you think, 'How's she done that?' She just does it without you knowing how she's doing it. It's like a swan, you know, she's paddling underneath, but it's the ease with which she does it." Producer Sarah Creasey agrees. "Paulette Randall is incredible. Her energy and presence—she's so awesome. There's something magical about her."

She really does have presence. Sitting opposite me in the fifth-floor green room dressed in flowing black with more silver bracelets on her arms and rings on her fingers than I could count, grabbing a bite of lunch while we talked because she'd very kindly given up the only free time in her day to talk to me, Paulette is the kind of person who makes you feel energised.

I first asked her how she approached a new script.

"The first thing is reading it and seeing how you feel," she says. "I think about what it does for me emotionally and if there's anything that I can draw on that I understand from that experience. Certainly in regards to that particular episode [18/35 'I'll Walk You Home'], I thought about losing people, death. And then I would ask the actors as well. The actors might have lost someone very close to them, someone they love dearly, but if not it's still an acting process, so it's about those characters and what they feel for that other character. I spoke to the DOP Peter Butler and I said this is my first time, so I don't know know how you camera-script and things like that, but I can talk to you about how I feel and how I think it should feel like and look like. He said, 'You just show me what you want and we'll shoot it, and if I think I can offer you something better I will.' So it was a bit on the fly, obviously with a lot of thought beforehand. But I'm not technically scripting it and regimented in that way, I kept it very loose in that sense and just wanted the actors to take us on that emotional journey they were all going on."

There are scenes in that episode that have a hallucinatory quality to them, where Arthur imagines he's talking to Chantelle, and he's walking through a strange version of an operating theatre in a hospital gown. "Coming from a theatre background I'm used to doing stuff that's not real in that sense," Paulette says. "Whereas Holby usually feels much more real. So for me those scenes were very exciting and I felt more at home doing that stuff, because I understood it more. So as long as the images work and make sense to you, then you can run with it."

Paulette is rightly very proud of that episode. "Whenever you're doing stuff and you learn from that, it's what you do next that counts, and I think you have to have faith. Of course you might do it differently if you could do it again, but if we could always go back and change things we'd never finish it would we? I was very happy with it, and surprised at some moments, because I was getting to know the cast as well as getting to know what I was trying to do with them. For me it was very successful. My sister lives in Spain and she doesn't really know the programme, but she watched it and she said, 'I didn't know who half of these people were and I was crying', and I thought, that's great."

I kept hearing around Holby that one of the directors was very squeamish and wouldn't even look at the surgery scenes on the camera monitor. It's Paulette.

"I can't even walk into the theatre set without my heart rate increasing and I get that pounding in my ears and I think I'm going to faint. It's the wrong show to be working on really!" she laughs. "I love it though. I have a lot of help when it comes to the operations and if I really can't cope I'll have already spoken to the actors so they know what I want. We've tried making the monitor black and white so I don't see it as red, and we've tried taping up bits so I can only see their faces, and that helps."

I wondered whether she'd visited the prosthetics department.

"No! That would be a step too far. They did say, why didn't I come and have a look, and it would probably alleviate my fears. I know where the prosthetics room is, but my head is always turned the opposite way when I walk down that corridor. I've never seen into that room. And I feel awful when I talk to those amazingly talented artists who work in that department, because it is extraordinary what they do. I have to say, I'm so sorry, you know I won't be looking at that but thank you so much because I know the work is amazing. Because people tell me."

She does go to the medical meetings, but finds it very difficult. "I can barely speak or listen in those meetings. It just makes me feel sick. I sit there fanning myself. I can't avoid going, though, because you need to understand how it should be done and if we need to adapt it, because we're not doing a documentary. Sometimes you need to speak to the actors about how they should be reacting to what's happening to them, so you need that information. It's the same with makeup and all of that, you have to understand what's happening to the patients physically as well as emotionally. I'm constantly saying to people, are we doing enough, is the breathing laboured enough, how uncomfortable would she be feeling, would she be able to bend over like that if she's had this done, things like that. So I try to make sure we honour the truth as much as possible without getting in the way of the story."

Holby isn't the ideal show for a director with an aversion to gory details, but Paulette loves it. "From being new they made me feel so welcome and were so encouraging and helpful, both cast and crew. Even here on the fifth floor with all the producers and the script department, everybody, they're just fantastic and really helpful and generous and approachable. It's a lovely environment to work in. I used to worry when people said it was like a family. You think, 'Well there are some families that are really dysfunctional!', but this one is great. And that's what keeps me wanting to come back, and thank God they've had me back."

After many successful years as a theatre director, Paulette says she wanted to have a go at directing for the camera. "I'm a bit of a Luddite and I'd always shied away from it. I'd worked in television before but always as a script editor or a producer. And I was script editing and producing comedy, where you have four or five cameras, which to me is like algebra and I can't do numbers. So I loved it and appreciated it and respected it, but I never really got it and never understood it, and knew it wasn't for me. But as I got older I thought, ultimately it's about telling stories and it's just another medium for that, so stop being so shy." She laughs. "But I can barely answer a phone and I can't type, so I know I have things about machines. Then I realised the foundations of theatre and television are the same—telling stories and getting people to perform."

She feels that she's learning on the job. "Instead of looking at it and thinking, 'Argh! I don't know what I'm doing!', I now kind of draw little pictures of each scene and where I think they're going to start and where I think they're going to move to. So I sort of do my own blocking as much as I understand it, and now I'm beginning to understand and do a little bit more of where the camera would need to be, but I'm still learning and still discovering what it can and can't do to make the story better. The rest of the team are fantastic. The DOPs, continuity and all of that won't let me get it wrong."

She also loves the editing part of the job. "Editing is amazing. I'm still getting thrilled by that, watching something and thinking 'I know what I can do in the edit with that'. It's lovely. I think ultimately it's about always wanting to challenge yourself as an artist. Fundamentally, I'm a storyteller, but you always want to see if there's another way of telling a story and another way of pushing yourself. It excites me more than it makes me nervous.

"It's a bit like when you're in theatre and you've rehearsed and rehearsed and then you get to the technical rehearsal when they finally get their costumes, and the lights and all of that and you know that all of those discussions you've had and those moves are going to work. And it's a nice thing to discover, that there are so many similarities between theatre and television, so as a director it's not that alien. I kept thinking TV's technical, with machines, and theatres are just people. When of course theatre has machines and gadgets too. I never looked at it in the same way."

Paulette talked about how her approach to TV directing is developing as she works on more Holby episodes.

"In TV and theatre I'm much more of an emotionally-driven director. I also like pictures, so when you relax and you're less nervous, you start to think, how about we do it through that window or what if the camera went there and we played around with it? As long as it doesn't get in the way of the story. As a viewer, if I'm too busy looking at that sort of thing and not listening to what the characters are talking about, then it's wrong. And there's a style thing that I guess I'm beginning to develop which is actually to keep things moving. Sometimes you've got no choice. If you're in the operating theatre there are certain rules—they have to stand on certain sides and it has to look authentic, but the rest of the time I think you can really play around with it, and it's about how you want your audience to feel, so whether it's really cutty and choppy or if it's a slow kind of build and more fluid. I don't know! There are directors here who've been doing it for years and they'd be able to tell you all the technical aspects. What I can tell you is knowing whether the story is working or not, understanding the characters' individual journeys, understanding the overall feel of that episode. I'm not an expert. Yet."

PROSTHETICS DESIGNER: MEGAN THOMAS

Next time you see blood pumping away you'll know there's
probably someone underneath that bed. – *Megan Thomas*

It's not often you walk into a room to be faced with a shelf full of legs. Male legs, female legs, hairy legs. One is too long for the shelf it's on and the foot lolls over the edge, pink and perfect with just a trace of hard skin on the sole. The shelf is labelled LIMBS.

Another room has photographs on the wall of burns, open wounds and guts. Someone is sitting at a bench carefully painting the most disgusting-looking ulcerous leg. There's a dead dog on the top shelf.

This is the somewhat unnerving prosthetics department at Holby, and if you've ever had to look away from a particularly gruesome procedure on the show, these are the people to blame.

The department might be unnerving, but the people who work in it are—as seems to be the case in every department of Holby—friendly, relaxed and knowledgeable.

Prosthetics designer Megan Thomas told me about her job. She reads the scripts, which already include the notes from the research team giving background information about the ailment or injury each person has. Megan attends the medical meeting with Holby's surgical advisers, who describe what everything should look like. She then goes online to look up the particular operation or injury and see what it looks like in real life. Her Google search history must be an interesting one. She's also observed real heart surgery and general surgery. "You have a new level of respect for surgeons when you're in there and see what they're doing. It's just mind-blowing." Needless to say, she isn't squeamish. "I don't think you could be, and do this job," she says.

It isn't always a case of faithfully reproducing what something would look like in real life. "Sometimes swollen eyes and faces and things like that could look a bit fake," Megan says, "So we use a bit of artistic license to make it look more like what a viewer would expect to see."

They also have to take into account what a pre-watershed audience can cope with. "It's trying to get the balance of showing what we need to without it being too graphic," says Megan. Even so, there have been scenes that have been cut because the injury or surgery portrayed looked "too brutal" in the edit. Megan says that's particularly the case with eye operations. One particularly disgusting-looking prosthetic was made for a storyline about a woman with an infection that was eating away the skin on her abdomen, so you could see into her stomach. In the end, it looked so horrific that it was only seen in glimpses. "Everybody was a bit grossed out with that one," Megan says.

When they've been to the medical meeting and decided what they need to make, a team of four people will be in the workshop making the prosthetics. They work on two or three blocks at a time and make whatever comes up. "Tomorrow we've got a neck operation. They're removing glass from someone's neck, so we'll be on set for that, and in the afternoon we're putting the piece on his neck to make it look swollen. Later in the week we've got a laparotomy where someone's stomach is cut open. We've got an aneurysm at the back so we have to move all the bowel and stuff away to get down and fix this aneurysm." Half the time is spent in the workshop making things, and the other half is spent on set.

The prosthetic pieces are all made of silicone. It starts off as a runny liquid in two parts or three parts, and when they're mixed there's a chemical reaction and it hardens. A swollen eye will first be sculpted in a material called Plastaline, or Monster Clay, and a mould is made from that. The mould is filled with silicone and that makes the actual piece. It's then painted to make it look realistic. Real hair is used for eyebrows or hairy chests and someone has to punch in every hair by hand. The finished effect is amazingly lifelike.

With each piece taking such a lot of time and effort, I wondered how much gets reused. Megan says it depends how it's being used. "Sometimes they get ripped, or sometimes it's something so specific to that character that we can't reuse it." Organs are often reused, but because they're so soft they tend to be fragile and don't stand up to much wear and tear.

In surgery scenes, the prosthetics team can sometimes make a prosthetic cavity that sits on top of the actor lying on the operating table. Other operations might need a deeper cavity, in which case it isn't possible to have the actor there, so it's all done in the edit—a shot of the actor's head, then close-ups of the operation.

You might remember 15/15 ('Push the Button Part 2' by Julia Gilbert) in which Arthur Digby accidentally snapped off someone's gangrenous toe. To produce the right effect, the team had to make an entire fake leg. The actor's real leg was hidden underneath the mattress and there was a hole made in the bed. This can't be done in theatre scenes because the beds used are special theatre beds, so a whole fake body is used instead.

Prosthetics are working on all filming blocks at the same time. They try to arrange it so no prosthetics are needed for the first week of each block, which gives Megan's department time to prepare. How long it takes to make a piece depends on its intricacy. When Elliot Hope had brain surgery (16/41, 'A Heart Man' by Rebecca Wojciechowski), the surgery took place via his nose. Prosthetics had to make a model of Paul Bradley's whole head. Megan was working on that particular model for a month. If she'd had nothing but that to do it would have taken a solid two and a half to three weeks just on its own. It involved making the mould, casting the head, colouring the skin and punching in the hair and eyebrows. The finished result was so stunningly realistic that nobody watching the episode would have realised it wasn't Paul himself. I've seen the finished head in the workshop and it was so lifelike it looked like it might start speaking.

Megan says that in prosthetic workshops people tend to specialise—there'll be someone who does nothing but sculpting, another who only does painting and finishing, another who will concentrate solely on hair punching. Because so many episodes are being worked on at a time at Holby, their prosthetics team have to be good at everything.

Megan's working day depends on whether she's going to be needed on set or not. She reads a lot of scripts and has to break them down and make notes about the prosthetics work required for each. She has meetings with directors and producers and the medical meetings. When not in meetings and doing paperwork she gets on with creating the prosthetic pieces, but because she has so many other demands on her time it tends to be the smaller pieces or things that aren't needed for a few weeks, so she can dip in and out when she has the time.

If it's a day when prosthetics are needed on set, someone from the team has to be there at 6.30am to apply the piece, and they stay with it on set for as long as it's needed. Sometimes a corner of a piece will start to peel up or move, so someone needs to be there to adjust it if necessary. For this reason, Megan occasionally has to ask the directors to take something out of the script, because it just isn't practical for a member of her team to be constantly on set.

The prosthetic is effectively another character in the scene and it can be quite uncomfortable for an actor to wear, so breaks are scheduled into the shooting. When Jules Knight (Harry Tressler) had a head and face injury in series 17, it took two and a half hours to apply the prosthetic and makeup to his face. He was unable to see out of one eye because of it, so he had to have a runner to help him get around. The prosthetic was difficult to remove, so shooting for those scenes had to be built around its practicalities.

Prosthetics work quite closely with the makeup department. If a character has a swelling, that's generally a prosthetic, but as the swelling goes down it will be the makeup department who have to create any related bruising or a cut.

One thing that I really wanted to know was how they got the blood to pump so realistically when the machines go beep in theatre (the beeping itself is a subject for another chapter). They use a pump like an industrial-sized garden-spray pump, which is attached to a little tube in the prosthetic abdominal or chest cavity and they pump up the pressure to make the blood pump. The blood itself isn't made at Holby because they use such large quantities of it, so they buy it in. There's a lot of sugar in it, and it gets very sticky.

When you see a beating heart during surgery on Darwin, it might ruin your viewing experience to know that it's quite likely that Megan or a member of her team will be underneath the operating table doing the pumping! They pump air into a little bladder to make the soft silicone heart look like it's beating. Megan showed me this by blowing down a tube into one of the prosthetic hearts and it was quite eerily realistic.

And what about the dead dog on the top shelf? He's been there so long that they don't really notice him any more, but he was the corpse of Elliot Hope's dog Samson, who was run over in 15/43 ('Digby Dog' by Martha Hillier). And don't worry—he's made of cushions.

SENIOR NURSING ADVISER: LISA SPENCER-BLACKSHAW

I think it's nice that Holby does a little bit of comedy.
When you work in the NHS there is fun, you do have a laugh.
– *Lisa Spencer-Blackshaw*

Jaye Jacobs (Donna Jackson) told me that one of the things she'd missed during her six years away from Holby was "having a nurse to talk to all the time. Because there's a nurse always on set and you just go, 'Is this something to be worried about?', and she goes, 'Don't be daft.'"

Chances are that this reassuring nurse was Lisa Spencer-Blackshaw, the senior nursing adviser on *Holby City*. She's been with Holby since the very first episode, after the producers got in touch with the hospital she was working at, Watford General, to see if any nurses there would be interested in advising a new show.

"I went in for the day and watched some filming, gave some advice on operating theatre instruments and equipment and went home," Lisa says. "I thought it was fantastic. Over the next few years I was rung up quite a lot and I'd go in on the odd day and help with filming and buying equipment. Then over the years it got bigger and bigger and we had to get another nurse because I couldn't do it all, then a third. And it's now been 18 years and it's been fantastic."

Currently there are three (real) nurses working on Holby. Each unit has a nurse attached to it and they advise on scripts, procedures and equipment. They're responsible for ordering the equipment you see in the operating theatres and showing the actors how to do things like put a drip up, take a pulse or put in stitches realistically.

Occasionally in operating theatre scenes you'll be able to see the nursing adviser—they'll be the ones handing the instruments to the 'surgeon'.

"The cast are handling real sharps, real needles and real scissors," Lisa says. "So if there's a nurse handing that to them it's safer. It helps the cast to perform the procedure if there's someone medically trained there who can say, 'Hold it like this, not this'. It just gives them that bit of professionalism if they're holding the instrument in the right way.

"We also look after the actor who's on the bed playing the patient. We can see them up close, keep an eye on them if they want to get up," she says, and explains that playing the patient in theatre is not an easy thing to do. "When you see the operating theatre scenes, the actor who is playing the patient is laying on the bed, below all the theatre lights, with maybe a prosthetic on their chest or their tummy, with a tube in their mouth for the breathing machine. It can be quite claustrophobic. They're covered with blue drapes and it gets very hot, so we have to have someone there keeping an eye on them."

Lisa addresses the frequent grumble that people recover unusually quickly from surgery on Holby. "It's true that somebody who has a heart transplant in the morning might not necessarily be sitting up chatting in the afternoon, but we've got an hour to show a patient's journey. I always think we just see snippets of the journey—you see the operation and then we see the recovery. It is quite quick though!" There is always a balance between getting the medical details factually correct and telling the story in a dramatically satisfying way. "We do really try to get it right, but we have to allow them to film as well. A good adviser lets them film the story and doesn't stand on set saying, 'This wouldn't happen'. We know that the stories are sometimes unusual or it's a very rare condition, but we go with that. We're there to try and make it look real."

Lisa or one of the other medical advisers will set up the operating theatre for a surgery scene a few days before it's needed for filming. The type of surgery and the equipment needed will have been discussed in the medical meeting prior to filming, where specialist surgeons advise on the specific procedure. "I check all the equipment. We might need scissors or a special instrument or just more swabs. We do all the stock like you would do in a hospital. All the heart monitors that you see on screen run off a simulator and the ventilator needs a cylinder of oxygen so we check that, so everything's working. On the morning of filming the prosthetics team will come up with their piece and put that on the operating table and at 8am the artists will come in and start rehearsing, and that's when we can practice with the instruments and the heart will beat and the lungs will move."

On the day I met her, Lisa had been setting up two different surgical scenes. "In Theatre 1, Darwin, it was a keyhole operation on the lung, so I've been getting that ready. In the other theatre it's a brain operation we're filming tomorrow, so that's a totally different set-up: microscopes, very fine instruments, very delicate. I get everything ready and help on the day with the filming."

On theatre-filming days, there's also a surgeon on set, who is experienced in that particular specialism, to talk the cast and crew through anything specific to the procedure being filmed. "Once we're ready, the cast will put on their scrubs and gloves and gowns, hats, masks, put some 'blood' on their hands depending how bloody the operation is, and start filming," Lisa says. "The suction you see is real suction. We also have a real diathermy which burns the bleeding vessels, so if you see smoke, that's what that is. We put a little bit of Vaseline on the prosthetic and touch that bit with the diathermy and that makes the smoke without damaging the prosthetic and it's safer. But the nurses always handle that because it can be quite dangerous."

The heart monitors that you see in Holby are simulators and they're similar to the ones used in hospitals for training purposes. "There'll be somebody sitting behind that machine holding on to the simulator and pressing a button at the right time, for when there's 'peril,' as we call it, or crisis. Somebody's heart goes from 80 beats to 120 and you can see that on the heart monitor. That's somebody pressing a button."

Megan Thomas has already described how the prosthetics team produce the beating heart effect, but Lisa explains that they also need to know at what speed to pump. "They know if the heart's bradycardic, which means slow. The prosthetics person would look at the monitor and see it going slow and make their heart beat slow. You hear 'He's tachycardic!' a lot, and that means the heart is beating really fast, so the prosthetic heart will be pumped really fast."

Another aspect of the job for the nursing advisers is to help the actors playing the parts of doctors and nurses to give a realistic portrayal. "Especially when they're in theatre for the first time," Lisa says. "They have to learn to stand in a certain way. They're handling the instruments and saying their lines at the same time. It's not easy. We also help them with how to say the medical words. The cast have minutes to learn the procedure. They don't get massive amounts of time to rehearse. But they're brilliant and I'm always impressed."

Lisa and her colleagues are still practising nurses. When they aren't involved in filming they usually go back to working in the NHS. "I will always go back to the NHS," Lisa says. "Operating theatres are my speciality and I love it. In theatre I can concentrate everything on making sure that the patient and the surgeons have everything they need, and to help with that operation."

Lisa enjoys taking this experience and expertise back to Holby. "I love anatomy. That's why I like the theatre scenes here—bits move, and bleed. The prosthetics are just stunning. And I love it when they've filmed a bit of surgery using the prosthetics, and when the advising surgeons come in they think it's real. We play them the footage and sometimes they say, 'Where did you get that footage? It's really good, really rare', and we say, 'It's not real'. So it fools the surgeons. I love it. I love the gore."

Working at Holby is also an opportunity for Lisa to extend her own knowledge. "In Holby we do tend to choose the weird and wonderful or the rare, so I have to have a really good look. I like learning procedures and protocol. Sometimes I learn new stuff here and find it takes time to reach the NHS department I'm working in. Holby's researchers are on the ball of the latest and newest thing, the latest posh machines and things. We don't always have those in the real NHS yet, though they are coming."

Lisa thinks Holby strikes the right tone in its depiction of hospital life. "You look at the news and it's miserable most of the time. Do people really want to see that again? Or can we make it a little bit more light-hearted and a little bit more fun sometimes? I think it's nice that Holby does a little bit of comedy. I love it, I roar at some of it, it's brilliant. When you work in the NHS there is fun, you do have a laugh."

Lisa genuinely loves her job and loves Holby. At one point when we were talking about it she affectionately stroked the wall of the room where we were sitting. "Mad nurse!" she laughed. "But this place runs through people's veins. We've seen babies born, sad times, really good times, weddings. I've got people here who came to my wedding. They came to my dad's eightieth, because he used to be a supporting artist here—he played a porter. Holby's so popular, wherever I go people are really interested in it. Everybody can relate to it, in a way. The NHS is so big and you're lucky if you don't know anybody that's been in hospital, or if you haven't been in hospital. All of my family and friends think it's great. I was really lucky to get this gig. It's a dream job."

SERIES MAKEUP DESIGNER: JO HOUTMEYERS

When it's HD you can see everything so you can't cake people
in makeup like they used to in the old days. – *Jo Houtmeyers*

Holby City hospital is well known for having the most attractive staff in the whole of the NHS. This is not just down to good genes and a blameless life—a little bit of expertly-applied makeup certainly doesn't hurt.

The makeup department at Holby is responsible for making sure the actors look good (or hungover, or ill, or whatever the script demands)—but there's a lot more to it than just wielding a blusher brush.

Series makeup designer Jo Houtmeyers told me that their day starts at 7am, and the first hour is the busiest. "There's seven makeup artists working in here at one time, so each person will have someone in their chair," she says. "So that's fourteen people in chairs or standing, and normally three or four shaving, cleansing, washing by the sinks." Men are generally in makeup for between five and twenty minutes, while women will usually take thirty to fifty minutes.

All the men have their own individual shavers and each cast member has a makeup bag of products which are only used on them. It's all colour-matched for them and takes into account their skin type and individual preferences.

The men get their hair cut every other week or every week if they have extremely short hair. Because each episode takes four weeks to film and various episodes will be being worked on at a time, it's important for continuity that the hair stays the same length.

At 8am everybody goes to the various sets and the room quietens down. It's Jo's chance to start reading through scripts. "Two weeks before they start filming I have a window to read the next two episodes. Then on Wednesday I go to the medical meeting where we've got real-life specialist surgeons and consultants. We can pick their brains on the surgeries we need. So if someone has a specific rash they'll say to us, 'It would be a very blotchy rash, but with little flecks of purple because of such and such'. So we try and get it as accurate as we can."

She also meets with the director to talk about the characters and whether there's anything she needs to note about their appearance—such as whether they're hungover. They also discuss the guest artists and where they might need a scar or tattoo.

Jo makes notes for each episode, which are then passed to the makeup supervisor for the block. The supervisor will do a scene-by-scene breakdown of every makeup note they need, so it can be quickly referred to—for example, in scene 45 this character has dirty fingernails, and in scene 46 they've been cleaned. Because the scenes aren't filmed in order, it's vital to keep track of all of those details.

Every item in every makeup bag has to be replaced when it runs out, so the department keeps a back stock of all the makeup and Jo orders more as necessary. There also has to be enough makeup for the guest characters. If a character is going to return in a later episode, stock kit has to be used so that the same makeup can be used when the character returns.

The department uses high-end makeup brands, because they need a good colour range and a long-lasting finish. They don't use one particular brand, though, because there isn't one that would cater for so many people's different needs. Some of the actors insist on vegan, cruelty-free makeup, others will need specific products for their skin type.

Jo says that for HD-filming makeup has to be minimal but very well applied. "You shouldn't see it, especially on guys. They should look believable. Obviously they're actors, they want to look good, so they're not completely free of makeup, but they shouldn't look caked." Having seen Bob Barrett and Alex Walkinshaw in their character makeup earlier that day, I can confirm that they didn't look made up at all—just nicely enhanced.

It's not just a case of getting makeup on people's faces and getting them out of the door. Jo says that in that first hour, every station in the makeup room will have a different atmosphere. "You've got the artist and the makeup artist in their little bubble in the morning. Somebody will be really happy and buzzing because something great's happened, so their conversation over there will be really upbeat and happy. Somebody over there might have had a late train—again—and they're moaning about that, and the makeup artist will be trying to cheer them up or calm them down. Somebody else will be sad about something. It is very much that each individual station has a different mood. We tailor how we deal with them, so we work around them rather than them having to work around us. We tend to follow their pace."

Each block of filming has three makeup artists working on it. Jo showed me a chart which has all the makeup artists colour-coded to show who was working with who. "On this block of episodes 24 and 25 we have Cara, Charlie and Tina working. Cara will always look after Matteo, Essie, Bernie and Morven on that block. Tina will look after the people colour-coded purple, and Charlie will only look after the ones in yellow." This is to ensure no single person is responsible for too many makeups and the workload is evenly and manageably spread between them.

The makeup artist will do the makeup for the person in the morning and then go to set with them and look after them there all day. If the makeup artist needs to go back to make up someone else, another makeup artist will look after "their" person until they return. Jo knows who works well with which actor and tries to put them with that person wherever possible, because she knows they do a good job and make that person look particularly good.

They keep a record of all the makeup notes—what each character used in every scene, how their hair was styled and so on. Scenes for one episode can be filmed weeks apart, so it's vital for continuity that all of this is recorded. It's all uploaded to the computer so they have an archive. If a guest character comes back they can look back and know exactly what was going on with that character. If they previously had an operation, they know that they'll need a scar and so on.

If a new character is coming in who has something specific they need, like a wig or a fake tattoo, they come in to the makeup department in advance to find the right wig or the right placement for the tattoo.

The makeup and prosthetic departments do cross over. While I was talking to Jo, a guest actor who'd been filming a scene earlier on AAU came into the room looking for the makeup artist he was working with. Jo explained to me that the character he played had a huge piece of glass stuck in his neck. "Prosthetics would have put the swelling on because it's a big swelling and there's something embedded in it. So they did that, then one of our makeup artists did the cuts on his face." As a general rule, things like skin discolouration, bruising, rashes, scars and small swellings are created by makeup. Anything that has to move, like a beating heart, or is particularly large and requires a piece to be stuck on, is prosthetics.

As we were talking, the phone kept ringing with queries for Jo. Then makeup artists and cast members started to file back into the room. One of the regular cast was ill, so filming had ended early. What had five minutes before been a quiet, empty room was now bustling with activity again.

SERIES COSTUME DESIGNER: HELEN ASHLEY

It might be fake blood and soup instead of vomit, but it all
has to go in the washing machine. – *Helen Ashley*

Helen Ashley has what for many people would be a dream job. She spends
a great deal of her time shopping for clothes. As Holby's series costume
designer, she has a lot of people to shop for and it's the part of the job
she enjoys the most.

"It's creating characters," she says. "You mention Sacha to anyone
and they always talk about his flowery shirts, or when Elliot Hope was
here people would always comment on his character ties. I find it really
important to make each individual character have something different to
everybody else."

She works closely with the artist to come up with a look that is suitable
for their character. "It's not just a question of sticking a shirt on or sticking
a top on, it's finding who these people are, who these characters are,"
she says. Sometimes one piece of clothing or one pair of shoes will give the
character the identity they need, so the job is also about understanding
the psychology of the character.

"Sometimes when they first start I'm the first person they meet, so
I do get very close with the artists," Helen says. "Everybody has issues

with their body, they don't like this or they don't like that and you have to work with them to get them to trust you."

She loves the shopping side of her job, but because Holby is filmed months in advance of when it's shown on TV, it can be tricky. Shooting Christmas episodes in August means that the shops aren't entirely full of Christmas jumpers when you need one. Christmas itself is the hardest time for clothes shopping, because the shops are crowded and everything is in the sales. Helen has to buy two of every garment and it's hard to find doubles on the sale rails. The reason doubles are needed is in the nature of the show—there's lots of sticky, sugary 'blood' around, or people get vomited over. It might just be soup, but it can still stain.

The fake blood has to be colour tested on the fabrics. To the naked eye it might look red, but depending on the lighting it might come up looking orange or brown, so it's tested whenever there's a change of camera or lens. Different types of 'blood' may react differently with the fabrics. Some types don't wash out so well, so new ones will have to be tried.

One thing that Helen absolutely insists on is that the majority of the clothes she buys for Holby are from the high street. She revealed to me that even Connie Beauchamp wore clothes from the high street, "And she always looked great in them". Helen says buying designer stuff would be a waste of money because viewers wouldn't be able to tell and it just isn't realistic for hospital staff to wear expensive clothes knowing they're going to need to be washed very regularly. "If you get the right style for someone you can get away with anything," she says. "It's just putting things together that work well. Some people do wear higher-end high street, but it'll be mixed with cheaper stuff as well." The exception to this is Guy Henry (Henrik Hanssen), whose suits have to be tailor-made for him because he's so tall.

Helen's daughter, who's now 14, has already developed an eye for what works with each character. When she's out shopping with her mum she'll say, "This would look great on Zosia", or "That's a Sacha shirt". Helen herself is never really off duty. On holiday in Australia once she spotted a perfect tie for Elliot Hope and had to buy it.

Like almost every other Holby department, the costume team's work starts with reading scripts and attending meetings with the directors.

They make notes about how the director envisages the guest characters in the episodes. The costume supervisors concentrate on the guest artists, while Helen focuses more on the regular characters.

When a new regular cast member starts, Helen finds out from the scripts and in discussions with Simon Harper and Kate Hall how they envisage the character. She talks with the artists about their ideas for the character and puts together a mood board, so everybody knows how the character is going to look. She loves the process of helping to create new characters, and enjoys being able to do something different. The wedding of Mr T and Inga (19/13, 'I Do I Do I Do' by Michelle Lipton) was fun because it involved actual designing of the Swedish costumes for the wedding, drawing them and having them made up. This was cheaper than going to Sweden to buy them. "Hanssen looked particularly lovely," Helen laughs.

She does have favourite characters to dress. Elliot Hope was always her favourite. "He would just go with anything and he didn't care if he looked slightly silly or slightly odd." Of the current cast, she enjoys dressing Jemma Redgrave (Bernie Wolfe). "She's got a really good figure to dress and she always looks great." She also liked dressing Mo Effanga, because her style involved a lot of bright colours and a very individual look.

One thing that Helen has noticed over the years (she's been at Holby since 2001) is that, style-wise, the actors will often start looking more like their character. "They'll suddenly start buying stuff that you're buying for them as a character. Everyone does it. It's almost like you've shown them something new that works for them, so they go and get themselves something similar." At first, actors might be resistant to some of Helen's ideas for their character. "They look at it and say, 'I'd never wear that', and I tell them, 'You're not wearing it, your character is'." She says that it often means encouraging people out of their comfort zone, and they're often pleasantly surprised.

Costume can be used to reflect aspects of character, a very obvious example being when Sacha had his mid-life crisis in series 19 and tried to change his image by wearing motorbike leathers. Helen says you start to recognise something as almost being a character's trademark look. "It can be the tiniest little thing, like the fact that Morven wears mustards and yellows and Essie wears pinks. And everyone recognises Serena by her coral shirts. She has a knitted doll in her room made by a fan, and other fan art that people have sent, all wearing the coral shirt. I love it because it gives her an identity."

The costume department consists of a series of rooms which are arranged on a long corridor. "This is my exercise," Helen says as she takes me from one to the other. "Walking down this corridor. Or shopping."

One room has all the costumes lined up and labelled for the guest characters who will be being filmed in the next few days. It's also where all the uniforms are kept. Down the corridor in the next room are the regulars' costumes, with the scrubs at one side, and their other clothes arranged on rails. I immediately spot Sacha's motorbike leathers from 19/9 ('Glass Houses' by Elliot Hope and Johanne McAndrew). At one side of the room is a lot of stock clothing. It looks like a well-organised jumble sale.

"Even though we shoot out of season, it's got to look like whatever time of year it's supposed to be," Helen says. "In the summer when we're shooting the wintry months and everybody's got to wear winter coats, they're not very happy. If we're shooting in January and February and it's supposed to look like April or May, everyone will be freezing and want to put coats and scarves on." The secret weapon in this instance is thermal underwear. Everyone has a set of silk thermals to wear under their clothing, and the long sleeved tops you see people wearing under their scrubs will often be thermals too. Even filming indoors, particularly on AAU, is sometimes cold in the winter.

There's a small stock room of spare clothing, which can be used if any of the supporting artists turns up in anything inappropriate. It's the first place Helen looks when dressing guest characters, because they might have something already that would work, before thinking of going shopping. Particularly noticeable garments wouldn't be used again, because eagle-eyed viewers might spot them and realise another character had previously worn them.

Helen thinks it's nice when viewers spot a garment they like and want to know where it's from. The reality is that by the time the episode is shown, the garment will have already disappeared from the shop where Helen bought it three months or so earlier. "The high street stores have such a big turnover of stock."

There's a laundry in the department which is constantly on the go and that's another reason why Helen doesn't believe in spending loads of money on the clothes. "It might be fake blood and soup instead of vomit, but it all has to go in the washing machine." The costume runner has the exciting job of doing the laundry—and masses of ironing.

PRODUCTION DESIGNER: GEORGE KYRIAKIDES

If somebody needs access to a window to throw themselves out of,
we need to make sure that's feasible. – George Kyriakides

The design department is responsible for the overall look of *Holby City*, from the colours on the walls to the furniture to the mobile phones the staff use. It has to have a consistent, recognisable look and it has to look realistically like a hospital.

"We try very hard to make it look real, which I think it does," production designer George Kyriakides told me. "We try to make sure, with the buyers, that all the equipment we use is the right sort of equipment and it's as up to date as we can afford it to be. The stuff we get is from companies that supply the NHS and other hospitals."

The NHS logo is used around the building and Holby has a deal with the NHS which enables them to use their logos as long as they don't change them in any way. "Recently there was a change in the way the NHS presented the name of the hospital and the NHS logo," George said. "It was a very small colour change, so we'll implement that as and when we need to update. We don't spend lots of money specifically in order to overtake the NHS in their graphics, but we try to keep up with them."

Design on Holby encompasses everything you see on screen apart from costume and makeup. This includes the sets. "If there's a new set we'll talk to the director and the producer to find out whether there's anything particular that we need to bear in mind," says George. "For example, if somebody needs access to a window to throw themselves out of we need to make sure that's feasible, so we don't provide windows that are too small for somebody to climb out of. It's got to be fit for the purpose of the script."

The layout of the fictional hospital is not the same as the layout of the sets (see the chapter *Holby is a Place*), so the department has produced a map for the directors to use which shows where the different parts of the hospital are supposed to be. "We have to make sure directors don't assume that Albie's bar is on-site," George says. "It isn't on-site because there's no such thing as a hospital pub! It's round the corner in the main street, but very often you have to remind people to make sure characters aren't seen in the hospital one moment and Albie's bar the next." This would mean a detail such as the character arriving at Albie's wearing a coat, so we know they've been outside. "We don't have an exterior for Albie's, although it has occasionally turned up in a script," George says. "If we wanted an exterior we'd have to build one, and we've got no space to do that. It's not important enough for us to do that.

"We've got three main wards and ancillary areas as well. When I first came here on series 13 we gave it an overall change of look. We wanted to make sure that each ward was identifiable by the use of colour, so AAU is basically very pale with bits of aubergine, Keller is blue-ish and Darwin is green-ish. You can't make the whole thing look green otherwise it looks like it's underwater, so we had to experiment with a combination of colours. In the past we've had an orthopaedics ward (in series 13 and 14 when orthopaedic surgeon Dan Hamilton was a regular character), which didn't actually exist so we had to create it from other spaces we already had."

I wondered how often Holby used locations rather than sets, and George said that, because 90% of the storylines take place in the hospital there isn't the same need for location filming that a show like *Casualty* will have.

"Occasionally you might see the characters at home, but not very often," he says. "We have one other studio where we can build people's flats or bits of their house." This is the area that was used to make Digby,

Dom and Zosia's flat, and then Isaac's flat afterwards. "We need to make sure the money we spend is worthwhile. If the script has a bedroom which is only seen in one scene, to actually build a bedroom is quite expensive when you add the costs of carpets, beds and wardrobes. You have to decide how important it is, so you always refer back to production to find out if they really want to spend £5,000 on one bedroom set."

A built set is still usually more practical than using a location, as George explains: "If the location involves a regular character, the likelihood is we'd want to go back again and again. Each time you use it you need three days to prepare, shoot and then put everything back to how it was. Now, anything can happen. Within any time at all those people can move out, it can be redecorated, so you'd have to start from square one again. So unless there's a guarantee you could go back year after year, or at least month after month, it can be tricky. The way we often get round that is by having exterior shots somewhere, then we match the interior in the studio, so we can keep the interior for as long as we like and we can use the exterior shots more than once, just to establish whose house it is."

George said that occasionally the streets around the Holby studios could be used for location filming—for example Shenley Road in Borehamwood was seen in the episode (12/22 'The Butterfly Effect – Part 1' by Justin Young) where Daisha Anderson was shot. When Sacha Levy married Chrissie Williams in 14/52 ('When Sacha Met Chrissie' by Justin Young), the wedding took place in the fictional Rodolfo's restaurant, which was often mentioned in the story. A restaurant in Shenley Road was used for the exterior and interior shots and you can see the 'hospital,' Neptune House, in the background when Sacha and Chrissie leave the wedding at the end.

The designers are generally given two weeks' preparation for a block of filming, but things don't always go according to plan. "There are times when the scripts aren't quite ready and you might have to start shooting without the script for the second episode of the block, so we get storylines drip-fed to us. There can be a bit of a panic, which we try to keep under control. But usually we get the final draft a week before we go to shooting, so you can plan for some things two weeks before. More often than not you work from early drafts in the first week and with a bit of luck the final drafts in the second week. On one of the current blocks (19/45 and 19/46 were being shot at the time) we've had to make a little model of a house. That takes a week to design, commission, make and have delivered. The schedules are always artist-led and as it happens they scheduled it for the first morning, so we had to have it delivered on the Sunday evening ready for Monday morning. It can be quite tight at times. As a design department I think we've always delivered on time. We seem to manage somehow or other, touch wood, to produce the stuff."

Everything you see on the screen—doors, windows, walls, carpets, furniture, telephones, lamps—is all generated by the design department, the props buyers and the graphics department. Graphics do everything like taxi signs, packaging on things such as books and DVDs that have to be invented. They've also recently revamped the Albie's menu. George told me that they'd been speaking to Kate Hall about whether Albie's itself was due a facelift. "You can't suddenly change the interior with no description in the dialogue, because the audience will be used to seeing Albie's as it is. It only takes a little line like, 'Oh look, they've done it up' or 'I hear it looks fabulous now. Even more fabulous than before!'"

Due to BBC rules, Holby have to be very careful about showing favouritism to any particular brand or product. All the characters have different brands of mobile phone, for example, so that it doesn't look like one brand is being promoted over another. Sometimes a fictional brand will have to be invented, like the Whippy Whirl Hanssen got from the vending machine in 19/30 ('Gold Star' by Ed Sellek). "The thing is with fictional stuff, everyone knows the brands around them, so you do end up having things like 'Bell Cola', which aren't quite believable," George says. "A Whippy Whirl instead of a Walnut Whip I can just about believe, but even then you have to be fairly careful. You have to make sure it's clearable. You can make a name up, but there might be something out there that already exists with that name, so it all has to be cleared and occasionally goes to the lawyers to make sure they're happy with it. It can take three or four days before you get the go-ahead, by which time they've probably shot the scene." This is why, when anyone uses a search engine on Holby they use 'Whippet Search' instead of Google. "If we used Google we'd get a call from one of their rival search engines saying, 'Why are you using them, not us?' You always have to strike a line between reality and acceptability. If a product is in the background and there's lots of other real products in the background, it's fine. Like in Albie's bar, there are lots of different types of beers, so if they've all got the same exposure that's considered acceptable, although you have to be careful all of those beers don't come from the same manufacturer."

Everyone in the design department is a freelancer. There's a company which is contracted to provide the carpenters, painters and other tradespeople as necessary. "We usually only have one chippy and one painter, but occasionally we've had to bring in more if there's a big new set going in," George says. The regular ward sets are constantly being upgraded to keep them looking fresh. "Whenever they're used you get scuff marks all over the place, you get equipment bashing into doors and things come away and fall apart, so you have to make sure everything's ready for the next block. So once they've finished shooting in Darwin the chippy and painter go up and look around to see if anything's been damaged. Continuity-wise you have to make sure you're not changing something that's suddenly not going to work. For example episode 50 is being shot after episode 51 because of the way the schedules are working, so there might be something in 50 that would have changed by the time you get to 51, so you need to work backwards and reinstate things. Everybody pitches in, it's in our interests to warn each other there could be an issue coming up. There's a lot of pre-planning."

The department also produces scale models of the sets and George showed me the model of Albie's. "This is so the directors can look through at the sight lines and make sure the shots they're thinking about are workable and won't show the top of the scenery. It's a useful thing for directors and lighting people to have."

One thing George likes about Holby is that the production staff listen to the art department. "In other shows they'll listen to cameras and lighting, but the attitude to the art department is, 'We'll sort that out in post-production'. We don't do that here because that would be more expensive, certainly on the schedule we run to. It takes up time and money, so we like to get things right at the start."

POST-PRODUCTION SUPERVISOR: ROBI BORGONOVO

I find it interesting how much you can trick the viewer into seeing something, but not actually show it. – *Robi Borgonovo*

Post-production supervisor Robi Borgonovo is the person who is responsible for each episode from when filming is finished until the episode is delivered for transmission. She books the editors, looks after the schedule for viewings and assembling and editing, and oversees the copyrights and clearances. She also does a lot of the compilations—the 'coming up' reels that appear on the BBC Holby website, and leaving reels for the actors.

The department consists of Robi, plus a post-production coordinator and two assistant editors, plus three editors working at any one time. Two will be assembling (making rough edits of the day's footage), one will be in fine cut (editing the episode for broadcast) and twice a year they employ a fourth editor to work on the standalone episodes.

The aim is to deliver the completed episode about two weeks ahead of the transmission date. After that it gets sent for subtitling, with a subtitling script provided by Holby, and also gets audio description added.

This whole process takes about two months, Robi explains. "Filming starts, and we start the assembly. So we have an editor starting just a couple of days after filming starts and every day they will assemble what was shot the day before, so that goes on for twenty days. Sometimes there's a bit of input from the director at that point, but some directors just want to concentrating on filming during the shooting period. They don't want to see anything that's been cut. Others want to come down every day and see how the material from the previous day has been assembled.

"After the filming's done we have two weeks for the fine cut, where the director will sit with the editor and will go through their own pass with the editor to make sure we have the version the director's happy with. And then it will go to the producer, the series producer and the executive producer.

"After all these stages, which take about six weeks, we have what is called the picture lock. At this point the episode goes through two parallel phases. We send it to the colourist for grading and to the dubbing mixer for sound. The grading takes only a day really. The sound takes just under a week per episode." On Holby, these two processes are done by brothers: the colourist is Vince Narduzzo and the dubbing mixer is his brother Mike. There's more about these processes in the following chapters.

"Once we get back the graded sequence and we have the final mix from the dubbing mixer we rejoin the two and we have a completed episode," Robi says. "Then we add the credits and captions and any effects that might be needed for that specific episode. Then it goes back again to the producer, the series producer and the executive producer for another check, because up to that point they've only seen a version that hasn't been dubbed or graded, so we want to make sure they watch the final version as it would go out. I do the eyeball check and it goes through a vid check for any technical specification and then it's ready for delivery."

One of the things that has to be checked is that the content of the episode is suitable for a pre-watershed show, in terms of the language used and the images shown. "It's a fine line between making sure we push the boundary as much as we can, but still within that pre-watershed specification," Robi says. If there are any grey areas she might send a scene or a whole episode to the editorial policy department at the BBC. They might request that a particular shot mustn't be held for too long, or something like a knife being used as a weapon can't be seen in close-up. "I find it interesting how much you can trick the viewer into seeing something, but not actually show it," Robi says. "So when somebody gets hit by a car, we don't actually see the impact. If you check frame by frame, we cut out before there is the actual hit, but because we see the consequence of the hit it gives the audience the impression they saw the actual impact."

It's often a question of intent. A scalpel being used to cut someone in an operation can be shown because it's being done to help somebody. A stabbing is intended to harm, so that would never be gratuitously shown or lingered on. Robi says there is some leeway, because there are occasions when there would be no other way to tell the story.

Robi has worked at Holby for 15 years, and has seen a lot of changes during that time. "When I started we were still filming on tape and we only had three edit rooms. We went from tapes to [computer] files, and then file-based delivery." Another big change has been the rise of social media, which has given Robi a new area of work. "Ten years ago I'd never have thought of doing compilations, but now we do the 'coming up' reels, the ones we publish every three months. It's quite fun for me to do them. It's more work, but it's fun, it keeps it challenging and interesting."

Like all jobs, there are bits of it that are less fun and for Robi it's all the paperwork she has to do. When the episode is delivered it has to be accompanied by all the information that's needed for any possible re-transmission. This includes making sure all the artists who worked on the episode have been listed, so that they get properly paid whenever the episode is retransmitted. The subtitling script has to be prepared. This differs from the shooting script because there might have been a reordering of the scenes, or sometimes the artists paraphrase a little bit and don't say exactly what's in the script. So in post-production they watch the finished episode and re-transcribe what actually happens in the episode. There are also notes for the audio description, because although the audio describers can see what's happening, they can't be expected to know all the medical terms.

On the subject of medical things, occasionally the editors need to check back with the research department to make sure everything medical seen on the screen happens in the right order, such as the different aspects of a surgical procedure.

Recently Robi has been compiling 'blooper reels' to go on the Holby website. "We realise the audience quite likes to see them, so now we're actually keeping them," she says. "Before, they would get deleted, but now we ask all the editors to keep them and we'll try to put out regular compilations. Not all of them are transmittable," she laughs. "And there aren't as many as you'd think. The actors take it all quite seriously. If you've been on set you'll see that there can be a bit of clowning around while the scenes are being prepped. It would be a long day if people didn't make some light relief. But as soon as it's on, it's on. So mistakes do happen but it's not like we get a selection every day, it's maybe once a week we have one or two. So we can maybe only manage a couple of blooper reels a year."

In the days when Holby was shot on tape, the tapes were kept because it was more of an effort to get rid of them than to keep them. Now that everything is stored electronically, every bit of footage that has been shot is kept up to the time of transmission in case last-minute changes need to be made. After transmission, a 'consolidated cut' of the episode is kept, in which there are a few additional frames either side of each shot that's been used in the final cut. This is to give some flexibility if the episode ever needs to be changed for future transmissions. This would be very rare, though.

"We had a few instances where music had to be changed because of some copyright law changes that had happened subsequently after transmission, but that's only happened a couple of times," Robi says. "So if we only had the final mix with the song already in it, we wouldn't have been able to change it. Luckily most of the music gets added in post-production, so it's not embedded in the shots. The alternative to being able to change it is to pay a lot of money! The BBC has a blanket agreement with certain record companies, so we just have to check whether the publishers and recording company are within the agreement the BBC has. If they're not, it would be costly. It's not that it's impossible to use tracks outside the BBC blanket agreement, but it just means you have to pay more. Then it becomes a question of whether it's editorially necessary for that specific song to be used or could we use something else that we don't have to pay a lot of money for."

Music is something that takes up a lot of Robi's time. "It takes me about three or four days of full-time work to find music for the 'coming up' reels that is clearable, because you want a certain mood to fit the picture. I tend to pick the music, though it sometimes gets vetoed. It has to have an emotional feel to it and I quite like songs with a bit of up and down to go with the drama side of the reel. The lighter side is easier to find, because anything quite happy and fast can work, but for the dramatic side it's a bit trickier."

She enjoys seeing the viewers' reactions to the 'coming up' reels on Facebook and other sites. "What we're trying to do in the reels is give a little hint of what might or might not happen—because we play. We don't want to give away all the stories! I like to see who people like, who they like a bit less. I pick little moments I think will be quite interesting or funny and put them all together. They are fun to do."

Robi says that even though she's usually watching episodes in disjointed form, she does try to watch sometimes as a viewer. "There are times to watch it for technical reasons, but there are times when I put audience glasses on," she says. "You have to remove yourself from the process of everything you know has gone on to make the programme by just watching and following the story." She remembers a scene in 18/31 ('It Tolls for Thee' by Joe Ainsworth). "Prior to Arthur Digby's death, it was when Arthur finally told Morven in the little multi-faith chapel what was going on and he showed her the scan. I was just watching the assembly, so that was the very first time I'd watched it. It was just three or four scenes and I was watching it on my computer and I started getting really emotional and started crying. Just at that point Eleanor [Fanyinka], who plays Morven, came in and she was like 'What's the matter? Are you alright?' and I said, 'You just made me cry!' After I explained, she was quite pleased she made me cry!"

Apart from when she's crying at emotional footage, Robi says she loves working at Holby. "I feel quite lucky every day when I walk through those gates. It's such a nice place. It's nice to feel part of a team and feel appreciated and it's a very collaborative programme to work on. I really love being here."

EDITING: ROB PLATT

If a camera was looking at you now with that bright window
behind you, the window would be Armageddon. – *Rob Platt*

"A lot of people think editors are purely technicians and just know how
to operate an editing system," says post-production supervisor Robi
Borgonovo, "But actually really good editors are very good storytellers
and there's a lot of creativity involved."

Rob Platt is one of Holby's regular editors, and does three blocks
of two episodes a year. I watched him editing a couple of scenes and
he explained the guiding principles behind what he was doing.

"Walter Murch, a film editor who worked on *Apocalypse Now*, wrote
a book called *In the Blink of an Eye*, about editing, that collates the
general rules that people have. His first three rules are story, emotion and
rhythm. The top of his list is: does the cut advance the story? Continuity
actually comes last. Other than someone physically disappearing from
a scene unexpectedly, things like what hand someone is holding something
in is bottom of the list of priorities." He mentioned a scene in the film
Batman Begins, where Maggie Gyllenhaal has her hand on Batman's face
in one shot, but on the other side of the shot the hand is not there. "The
whole scene is played like that: the hand is on, the hand is off, the hand

is on again. I would doubt very much on a feature film that they didn't have an option to fix that but they obviously prioritised the emotion of the performances over continuity."

Nevertheless, it is important not to confuse the audience with bad continuity, and one area where this becomes an important issue for editors is where the actors in the scene are looking. "When someone looks at something or somebody, my instinct is I want to see what they're looking at. So that's generally one of the things I use to help me tell a story and for me to feel happier with a scene," Rob says.

The scene he was working on that morning was from 19/43 ('The Evolution of Woman' by Simon Norman). It featured a character called Julie (played by Tracy Wiles), who had been dating Sacha. She was talking to a patient in Keller. Sacha, Dominic, Essie and Lofty were standing by the door watching her and talking about her. As Julie moved from the bedside to go over and talk to the group by the door, Rob explained that it was a difficult scene to edit, because of where each of the characters was looking at any particular moment. "She's talking to Sacha there, so that cut works. Sacha is looking left to right, she's looking right to left." He showed me what the scene would look like if a different shot was used, and it did feel odd because Julie seemed to be looking at Dominic while she was meant to be talking to Sacha. "In most instances the scene will be played in its entirety from almost any angle, so then it's up to the editor to decide when to go from the mid-shot to the close-up. We usually start with a wider shot and tend to use the close-up for the little bits of detail so you get emotionally drawn into it."

He carried on editing the scene and showed me where he would cut from a close-up of Sacha to Julie. "I see Sacha turning and I want to know what he's looking at and what the other person is doing at that point. Also cutting to Julie keeps her involved in the scene and maintains a nice rhythm."

As the short scene progressed, Rob felt he wanted to add a shot of how Dominic was reacting to something Julie had said. "I'm just going to put in a little bit of time just for that to happen. It's just half a second, but you have to squeeze things apart to get all the little moments you want in, otherwise it ends up as a little bit of a car crash."

"If we add too many of these pauses it ends up being a much longer episode than we can transmit," Robi Borgonovo added. "So we'd have to adjust something somewhere else, but that's something that gets decided in fine cut with the director. It's more concerning if it goes under time. If we end up with a fifty-minute episode that's not good enough. Ideally we aim for sixty-three or sixty-four minutes at this stage."

In the scene Dominic leaves and Essie pulls Lofty away so Sacha can talk privately to Julie. Rob wanted to show a bit more of Essie and Lofty in close-up, but Lofty wasn't looking in quite the right direction. "It's not quite right when you look at it under a microscope," he says, "But actually your eye is drawn to Essie because she's the one who starts to move, so you can get away with that cut. What I tend to do is put it together quickly to see how I think it makes me feel, so by then you've created a structure for the jigsaw. Then I watch it to see if I feel I'm missing anything, and then quite often I'll then do due diligence and look through all the different shots and think if I've missed anything the director wants."

At the end of the day Rob will have assembled five to seven minutes of material, which he then sends to Robi and the episode's director, producer and script editor. The scene described above was just under two minutes long when finished, but for that Rob had twenty-four minutes of footage to work with. He colour-codes the clips to make it easier to find what he needs—for example, every close-up on Sacha would be colour-coded pink, Dominic would be light blue and so on.

He started working on another scene, which showed Morven in the Victorian corridor of AAU talking to a male guest artist who was sitting on the floor. "Scenes arrive in the order they've been shot, but I tend to try and edit them in episode order because that might make a bit more sense for my day," he said. The first thing he did was to quickly go through the shots he'd been given for the scene, which show up on his computer as thumbnails, applying his colour codes and looking at the director Tracey Rooney's notes to see if there was anything she'd specifically highlighted. "You tend to look at the director's preferred takes as your first port of call. Or sometimes you get a note saying, 'Look at everything', in which case you end up going through it line by line and looking at every slate. Which you sort of end up doing anyway."

As Rob worked on the scene he explained that the actors had been trained to leave a minuscule gap before they speak, specifically to make editing easier ("get the scissors in" as he put it), unless it's a situation where they might be talking over each other, in an argument for example. "Overlapping is great, as long as they stick to the script, because what they tend to do in the heat of the moment is they'll all overlap each other's dialogue and if they've switched the wording around from one take to the next the editing is an absolute nightmare. That's when Robi hears me swearing across the corridor because you've got this jigsaw puzzle that's becoming impossible to put together. Where your instinct tells you you want to make an edit, you can't make it, and then continuity can get messed up. Then you decide it all works in a wide shot anyway because it's easiest."

The editor in a way is trying to replicate the way we would look at things in a normal conversation. Rob explained it to me this way: "If Robi's just said something horrible about you, I might be looking at you fairly sharpish to see how you're reacting to that insult, whereas if Robi's speaking and you're just watching casually, then there's no reason to focus on you unless Robi looks at you, and then I'll look at you. I'd have no reason to look at you unless there was a question being asked or you were doing something interesting."

One thing that kept being mentioned was grading, which is the job of colourist Vince Narduzzo. The timespan of an episode will be a couple of hours to a couple of days. This will be made up of footage that has been shot over three weeks, in different lighting conditions and at different times of the day. The director of photography tries to keep the lighting consistent, but it's unavoidable that certain shots will look different to others. The colourist makes the whole episode look homogenous, so you wouldn't think one shot was lighter or darker than the others. The tone of the picture can also be made a little warmer or cooler as necessary.

When you see the footage from the camera on Holby, the picture looks washed-out and milky. This is because what comes from the camera is called a Log C image. This is a process by which the camera captures the whole of the image, unaffected by very bright areas or very dark areas. "If a camera was looking at you now with that bright window behind you, the window would be Armageddon," Rob said. "You wouldn't see any buildings or roof behind you, it would just be a white mass. When they shoot Log they're trying to protect the dark parts of the picture and protect the light parts of the picture. Essentially it's preserving all the information. That can be bent back again by a basic grading tool to give back some of the depth of the colours and then fine-tuned by the colourist. What Vince [Narduzzo] the colourist tends to do is, because all the sets are blueish, he tends to pull it all away from the blue a little bit. He's got a much more sophisticated tool than we use. A colourist is lighting after the fact, basically."

DUBBING MIXER: MICHAEL NARDUZZO

If it wasn't mixed it would be quite noticeable. It would
sound not like Holby. – *Mike Narduzzo*

You've probably never even thought about why and how Holby sounds like it does. I hadn't either until I spent an absolutely fascinating morning with Holby's BAFTA-winning dubbing mixer, Mike Narduzzo.

He works in a large studio, sitting behind a complicated-looking mixing desk. There's a big screen in front of him to watch the episode he's working on, which is flanked by massive speakers. When the heartbeats play at the start of the theme tune, the sound is so deep it vibrates the floor.

Mike talked me through what he was doing as he worked on the opening scenes of an episode. He receives the final edited version of the episode. Each track of sound is depicted on his screen, and a line shows where each edit has been made. Every time the sound has been cut, Mike has to make sure it doesn't sound like it's been cut.

The big screen showed an opening scene (from 19/20 'What We Pretend to Be' by Owen Lloyd–Fox) in Pulses, featuring Marc Elliott (Isaac Mayfield) and guest artist Debra Stephenson talking at the counter. Because of the way the voices were originally recorded, her voice was very loud compared to his, even though they were standing next to each other in the scene. On Mike's computer screen it was easy to see the difference in the sound levels as a graph. He adjusted it and the scene sounded normal and natural.

Mike is so used to this work and is so attuned to it that he spots every tiny thing. Debra Stephenson said the word "slow", but two versions of her saying it had been edited together, so on (very) careful listening it sounded like she was saying "s-slow." Mike fixed that too, because he's a perfectionist. "It's very small, but it's not right," he said, cutting and pasting to get rid of a tiny click he'd heard on the soundtrack.

With the script in front of him, he knew that Isaac's phone was about to ring, although there was no ringing on the soundtrack. He added the ringing sound, having to place it very precisely so that the ring sounded just before Isaac looked down to answer it. Mike's computer contains a library of hundreds of sound effects. "If the phone sound wasn't there you would wonder why," he says. "Now it is there, you don't think anything about it. I spend my entire life making sure no one can hear what I've done."

The muffins might be real in Pulses, but the coffee machine isn't— or it isn't actually used, anyway. The sound of coffee brewing is also one of Mike's sound effects. Trying to fit it into the scene in the short gap between Isaac asking for coffee and the cup being placed on the counter wasn't an easy task, however, and took several attempts.

Remember that the lift in the entrance area isn't really a lift, and the doors are hand-cranked by someone in Pulses' cupboard? The actual sound of this is like a barrel being rolled down a metal slope, nothing like a lift at all. When Mike started work at Holby he went up and down in the Neptune House lifts with a recorder and got all the sounds of each floor, the beeps and the voice saying "Lift going up" etcetera. It's this that you hear when anyone uses that lift near Pulses, or any of the lifts, with Mike adding the sounds exactly at the moment each one should happen.

In the scene we were watching, Isaac was talking on the phone to Dominic, and as the action cut from Isaac inside the building to Dominic outside in the garden, Mike made the sound of the lift voice seem to be coming out of Dominic's phone, so we were hearing what he was hearing.

To do this he used a graphic equaliser, turning off the bass to make the voice different with a preset 'telephone' setting.

Unlike almost everybody else who works on *Holby City*, Mike doesn't look at scripts in advance. When he gets each episode to work on it's the first time he'll have seen it. "I actually enjoy watching it as I'm doing it," he says.

Each episode can take between three and seven days to work on, depending on the content. Episodes based in the hospital are easier than the stand-alones shot on location, because on a location shoot the sound recordist may have had to cope with being in a busy, noisy place and they have a lot to shoot in a short time. These episodes can sometimes take two weeks of work, depending on whether there's a lot of dialogue to re-record.

On the day I visited in early December 2016, Mike was working on an episode due to go out in late February 2017, so he was about nine weeks ahead. There is always the possibility that last-minute changes have to be made, and Mike said it has happened that someone has come running down the corridor with an episode due to air that night. On one occasion, by coincidence a character in the show who had been stabbed had the same name as someone who got stabbed in real life. The scenes involving that character had to be recut so the name by the bed wasn't visible and then the actors had to come in and re-record any dialogue where his name was mentioned, using a new name that was as close as possible so it could be synched with the lip movements if it wasn't possible to avoid seeing their faces as they spoke. Only that morning Mike had an email from Oliver Kent to request that a character who originally said "Jesus" could come in and re-record it, changing it to "Jeez".

As well as taking stuff out, Mike has to add stuff in. "If I remove the dialogue in a scene where they're walking about, I also lose the sound of their feet as well, so I've got different shoes down there, including size 10 heels, which I can walk about in on different surfaces to record the sound." In a cupboard he has small pieces of concrete, hospital floor and other surfaces he can record himself walking on. He also has a bundle of scrunched-up video tape and cassette tape, and this is used to produce the sound of walking on grass or leaves.

He showed me this in practice in the Mr T and Inga wedding episode (19/13, 'I Do I Do I Do' by Michelle Lipton). In the scene where Mo arrives at the wedding, originally there were already some rustling sounds where Chizzy Akudolu was walking on the grass, but a lot of the sound on the finished article was Mike in his heels walking on videotape. The episode was set in January and had to have a wintery feel, so Mike added the sound of winter birds such as rooks. Nobody would ever have noticed it, but hearing the scene without it and then with it, it did add to the atmosphere. When the cushion with the rings on it fell into the water and Mr T fished it out, the sounds of the water dripping off it were added by Mike from his library of sound effects.

Jac and Ollie were seen getting into a taxi to come to the wedding. It was decided that their conversation should continue after they were in the taxi (although they couldn't be seen), so Rosie Marcel and James Anderson came to Mike's studio to record the little bit of improvised dialogue where Jac asked Ollie if he thought there'd be a free bar at the wedding.

When the dancing at the wedding scene was filmed, there wasn't any music playing. A section of music was played for the actors to give them the rhythm they'd be dancing to, but the dancing itself was done in silence. This is because if there's music playing it becomes impossible to edit the scene. Mike added the music afterwards, and he also added some noise of dancing feet. Mike keeps an archive of sound effects from all the jobs he's worked on and the dancing sounds actually came from effects he used for the ballroom scenes when he worked on the comedy *Hi-de-Hi!* in the 1980s.

Until Mike works his magic on the operating scenes, those emergency moments when the machines dramatically start going beep are actually rather quiet. There's no beeping, no squelching and no suction sounds, for the same reason as there is no music—it would make the scene impossibly difficult to edit. So all of that atmosphere is added in the dubbing mixer's studio.

In every hospital or public place there's a background hum, of footsteps, talking, coughing, doors opening and closing. Things you wouldn't notice until they weren't there, when the silence would make things seem very peculiar indeed. Mike has a different set of background sounds for each ward. He got 10 or 12 supporting artists to go around the ward sets walking, talking quietly and coughing, and recorded that. They had to be careful not to say anything specific and make anything sound like a repeating pattern that viewers might notice. They did the same in the stairwell for background noise at different parts of the stairs.

Inspiration can arrive at any time. When Jonny Maconie was in prison (17/23, 'We Have the Technology' by Nick Fisher), Mike happened to be in St Albans Abbey and realised the sound in there would be perfect as the background sound in the prison. He recorded five or ten minutes of the ambient sound in the Abbey, a background hum with distant voices and banging noises. He played it for me and it sounded echoey, like something underwater, and strange. "Depending on what level you play it at, it can be all sorts of different things," Mike explained. So while you were watching a prison, you were actually hearing a church.

Mike works very much on his own, and this is partly due to advances in the technology he uses. "When I first started mixing it involved about eight people. There were dubbing editors, producers, directors, but now there's just me." Every couple of weeks a director will come and sit with him to watch the episodes he's done and give notes. There are also the times when the actors have to come down to record additional dialogue, or re-record lines that weren't clear in the original recordings. Mike likes it that he's his own boss. "Everybody else in this place works with somebody else. I'm very lucky that I don't have anybody breathing down my neck. This sort of programme used to take three weeks to do with three or four people working on it. When I came here and I was able to do a programme a week on my own they were very happy!"

ON THE SCREEN

DAVID AJAO (DAMON FORD)

You get to a really emotional part, but the thing that's made you emotional hasn't been filmed yet. – David Ajao

David Ajao plays Dr Damon Ford. His first episode was 19/35 ('The Hard Way Home' by Nick Fisher). I met him a couple of weeks before that episode was screened, so he didn't yet know how his character was going to be received by the audience.

"When it comes to being with the cast and being on set I don't feel new any more," he told me, "but in terms of the show I haven't even had my first episode yet. It feels like I'm part of everything, but I'm not out there yet. We've filmed some great stuff so far, so hopefully it goes down well."

He described his Holby character as "young but really strong-willed. He works really hard but often puts his foot in his mouth. He forgets he's supposed to be really professional in that environment and he'll go and mutter stuff which is completely harmless. He gets ahead of himself sometimes, but he's a really loveable guy. People realise that everything he does comes from such a good place and he has a kind heart".

Speaking of hearts, Damon has a genetic heart problem called hypertrophic cardiomyopathy, and this is part of who his character is.

"It's always in the back of his mind because in the past it's held him back somewhat," David says. "He had to take time out of school, so he had to work extra hard to get him to the place he's in now. It comes across as him being really determined and wanting to help people because he's had that past experience himself."

Holby is David's first regular TV job. "You come in and everybody knows what they're doing. To come in and just jump on the train everybody else is on was a little bit daunting, but they made it so easy. I'd met Chizzy [Akudolu, Mo Effanga] before and I've known Ellie [Fanyinka, Morven Digby] for six or seven years and I'd worked with Hugh [Quarshie, Ric Griffin] on the *Othello* he did a couple of years ago, so I was familiar with people, but you're coming onto a set where you've got the grips, you've got runners, different ADs, the SAs…I thought I needed to make sure I nailed it because I didn't want to be the weak link in such a well-oiled machine."

His first few scenes were with Christian Vit (Matteo Rossini), who managed to put David at his ease, as did director Tracey Rooney – "She was so open and calming." David told me he already felt like part of the Holby family. "What I love is that even the seasoned actors who've been in this show for however many years always have an ear if you need to talk about something. They will always come up to me and ask how I'm doing, and ask me if I want to know anything. Sometimes you go on jobs and you might not speak to people, they might just go off to their dressing room and they'll only see you on set. But here it feels that everyone is open to talk and to come together to create something special."

To prepare for his part David binge-watched lots of episodes to get the feel of Holby. "I wanted to make sure I know the world we're creating and what would be my role in that world, rather than just coming in as a single entity," he says. "You have to be able to get with the pace of the show." He was surprised to find how long it takes to make an episode. "My first episode started filming in the middle of February and it's not out until June. There's so much work that goes into it that you don't see as an audience member. I feel like people have a passion for it, from the producers to the ADs to runners to SAs, everyone wants to make a great show and they really care about it. I think that really shines through."

When David auditioned for the role he'd already done extensive preparation and had lots of ideas about who his character was and where he was going. "I like to go away and work on it and really create the character before we even get in the room, so even if we don't have the same idea for the character I can come with something to talk about and we can discuss, rather than just come in with the lines," he says. When he met Kate Hall and Simon Harper he said they filled in the blanks about how they envisaged the character. "A lot of what they said was reinforcing my views, so we were on the same page," he says, but he then had a week and a half before filming started and didn't hear anything else about whether they'd thought his ideas for the character were what they wanted. "Then when I came in to start, Kate said they'd loved what I did in the audition and thought I'd got the right idea, so it was all fine."

He got the script for his first episode three days before he was due to start. "I was bricking it!" he admits. "You don't realise how much you're going to have to learn until you're in week three and you've got three scripts and you're almost finished with one, but then you're starting the other block. It was a shock to the system! Luckily I'm all right with learning lines."

The pace of filming required by Holby was something David had to get used to quickly, coming from a background of doing mainly theatre, where he could be spending six months in rehearsal and creating a character. "You get to a really emotional part, but the thing that's made you emotional hasn't been filmed yet," he says. "There was one day when I was working with [director] Jamie Annett and we spent the day going over something which had nothing to do with what was coming up. It got to half past six and I had to do a really emotional scene and we only had 30 minutes to do it in. I'd been in the whole day, filming in every scene and he said, 'Right, you know what's happened previously in the text and you've just got to go there'. I was so drained from the day I didn't know how to get there, but you train your mind and you just push yourself. I remember going away into a corner and not speaking to anyone— because usually I'm a loudmouth on set, I can't help but go around and make jokes with everyone—but at that moment I knew I had to take the time to actually go there. It was really hard. I had to work this picture up in my mind of what had happened, even though we hadn't filmed it yet, and just go with it. And it was great, I managed, thankfully. But it was a shock to the system. In your mind you're arranging all these pieces of a puzzle. You've always got to be aware of the things that have happened, even if you haven't filmed them yet, so you work out the whole journey prior to starting filming so you can jump into it and know exactly where you are."

To help with this process, David spends a lot of time dissecting a new script and he keeps all of his scripts in case he needs to go back and look at how his character was at some point in the past. "It's important to look at previous episodes to see how that's going to influence you going forward," he says. "But keeping the scripts will probably start getting annoying soon, because I'm running out of space!"

David says watching Rosie Marcel (Jac Naylor) work has been especially helpful for him. "She's such a professional. Watching how she's so on point with where her mark is, where the camera is, she's got the character down, she knows exactly what she's doing. She even makes little subtle changes to the script when she realises something doesn't work, medically, you can't say this or that. Seeing how involved she is in the whole process has really helped me. Because I'm still learning and still picking things up, to come in and see someone who is so aware of her surroundings and the text and the other actors, that's been brilliant to see. And she's been really supportive of me as well, which is great. I love seeing someone so dedicated and so intelligent with their craft as well. I've had some really great scenes with her where Jac's just shut Damon down," he laughs. "She plays it great and as soon as the camera stops, Rosie's back and she's really lovely. As Jac she's super-scary, especially for Damon. He admires her, because he wants to learn from brilliant minds, but she scares him a little bit."

I wondered whether David would be watching his first episode. "I don't know. I'm really bad at watching myself, it weirds me out," he said. "But my friends and family have said we should have a get-together to watch it, so I think I'm going to get roped in, but we'll see."

One thing he hadn't done was go to post-production to have a look at how he was coming across in the edits. "I always feel that I'd know if I've done something terribly wrong, plus I trust the directors to let me know if it's not working. The after bit doesn't quite excite me as much as being in it. I love the acting side of things, but the watching back is a bit scary for me. Maybe I should watch a bit more to see how I come across on screen, but I don't really like looking at myself. I can barely look in the mirror! I have a very quick routine in the morning—no sleep in my eyes? Great. And I'm out. I'm the quickest in the makeup chair, though I do get my hair cut every week. I'd like them to leave it one time so it looked like I grew an Afro from one scene to the next," he laughed. "Yeah, that can happen. My hair grows really quickly!"

David said he was definitely already part of the Holby family. "It's so much fun. There are moments when it gets stressful, but I've been on sets before and I feel that some of the best work is done when people are happy and working together. On Holby that happens all the time. People know each other and how each other works and relationships that are built over time can produce some really great things, because people start to understand each other a lot more. I think Holby has that in abundance. It's such a team, such a family."

DAVID AMES (DOMINIC COPELAND)

You can't just have fifty-two blissful hours.
It just wouldn't work. – *David Ames*

David Ames was the last person I spoke to for this book, and when we finally sat down for a chat he'd just finished location filming for the standalone episode that centred on the wedding of Zosia March and Oliver Valentine (19/50 'Veil of Tears Part 1' by Joe Ainsworth).

"Being on location is always a pleasure," he told me. "We all spend so long in these buildings, every day for twelve hours a day, so when you do get thrown a little bit of location stuff it's like a different job."

Filming took place at Brocket Hall in Hertfordshire, which has been used several times for Holby weddings, including the Effanga wedding standalone (17/13 'Brand New You' by Rebecca Wojciechowski). "It's just stunning," David says. "It was lovely to have a good week or so just turning up to those kind of views every morning. At 7am trying to wake yourself up with a coffee, it was gorgeous to be stood there. The inside of the place was absolutely stunning as well. There were ornate paintings throughout it, beautiful furniture, all very grand."

The storyline was bittersweet for David, because it marked the end of Camilla Arfwedson's time on Holby. "I'm sure as people know Rob [Ostlere] and Camilla and I became thick as thieves on the show, both in character but more so outside the building," he says. "We'd spend twelve hours a day with each other, travel to work together, travel back home and then we'd be like, 'Shall we go for a drink?' We couldn't spend enough time with each other.

"In the wedding episode Camilla and I have a beautiful little scene, which is me helping her get ready for the wedding. It was the last scene we filmed together, so there were heightened emotions for both of us. Camilla and I like to chew a scene over before we do it and change it a bit if there's something that's not quite landing properly. In this scene I had to ask her which shade of lipstick she wanted and she was meant to go, 'I don't know, whichever one'. I said to her I thought it would be better if she asked me which shade of lipstick she should use and I knew which one to hand to her, so it was like we'd done it before, I'd sat with her getting ready before. It's about us knowing each other so well. We thought it worked brilliantly and the director said he liked it because it showed our closeness. It just adds a certain intimacy and poignancy to it which is really lovely."

Back in the everyday routine of filming at Elstree, David described how he gets into character for the day. "I'm always early," he says. "There's nothing worse than running late and having to rush through everything and go straight on set. My brain can't function like that. So I'll get in, grab a coffee and sit in my dressing room for a bit. My call time is usually 7.20 or 7.30am to get to makeup. I have a shave, wash my face, moisturise, then have my makeup done, then I'll go and put my costume on. Then you get on set, say your good mornings to everyone, then we go straight in for a line run at 8am of the first scene of the day, after which you block the scene with the director, then we rehearse it enough times so we can then do a crew show. We bring the crew in and they watch everything and see what needs to be done throughout the scene, so makeup work out if they need to do any makeup on any prosthetics or anything like that, and the same with costume. Then they can light the scene and the camera crew will get their stuff sorted. So that's my little window where I'll go and sit and eat a yogurt or something and go over my scene and slowly but surely work out where I need to be through the day, emotionally."

Scenes are not necessarily filmed in the order they come in the script. Sometimes scenes from later in the episode are filmed first. "It's not like theatre where you begin the play and emotionally have a journey to get through. You can begin the day being heightened, being emotional or angry or let down, and then at the end of the day you have to pretend you've not done any of that yet. So you have to erase it from your mind and then do a scene where you don't know what's coming," David says. "You have to be quite adept at switching your emotions on and off, as and when."

He says that can sometimes be difficult. "There have been times when I've had to say, 'Just give me five minutes, I need to be on my own for a moment.' Particularly around the time of Arthur's death, and the tumultuous relationship with Isaac, I found there were times when I had to step away and go and have a moment to work out where I am in this particular scene and work out what it is I need to be doing and what it is I need to be showing or not showing. It can be quite exhausting to do that, especially when you're doing a scene where you have to get really upset and you have to hit that every time. Even if the camera's not on you and it's on the other person, you need to be able to hit it for them to be able to react. It can be quite confusing at times as well. You're thinking, 'So what happened before this?' But we'll have the continuity person there who'll be able to say, 'The scene before this is the one we did yesterday and the one that comes after is the one we did a week ago outside', so you can piece it together. It's like a jigsaw with pieces of sky and pieces of ground and the little bits in between. It takes a while to fill it all in, but once it's done hopefully the picture makes sense."

David thinks the energy on set is definitely helped by the family atmosphere. "When guests come into the show, the number of times they say it's such a lovely environment, such a lovely bunch of people. We're all very proud of the environment we create and it's through wanting to do the best for the show and being proud of the show and the work we do here. We all love being here. That's why we do what we do. Some people just blend in beautifully, like when Marc [Elliott, who played Isaac Mayfield] came and joined the show. No one had the smallest negative thing to say about Marc at all, he was wonderful and just so full of life. The first scene of the day he'd always be, 'Come on! Right! Let's go!', and he'd be raring to go, which is wonderful."

It was just as well that Marc and David got on so well in real life, because the storyline they had to play out, about Dominic being abused by Isaac, was intense and difficult. "I knew from the outset that it was going to lead to somewhere emotionally damaging and they'd hinted towards it being physically harmful," David says. "It was such a long storyline and they played it really well, with little things sown in here and there, just to allow people to go, 'Oh. That's not quite right. He's not quite right'. The way Isaac would emotionally bully and belittle and play with and toy with, and it got to the point where it was becoming more and more evident, and then it reached the point where it was really quite obvious. Then just as Dom plucked the courage up to say, 'No, get lost', that's when Isaac went for the punch, which floored Dom both physically and emotionally. It made him fearful and that's when he really felt like he didn't know what to do.

"One of the directors here, Jennie Darnell, who is wonderful and one of my favourite people, pointed something out to me in a scene once. It was when we were in Albie's when my parents had first met Isaac and my mum Carole cottons on that something's not right [19/14 'Aces High' by Joe Ainsworth]. Just as they leave, in the script Isaac says, 'Another drink?', then he gets up and goes to the bar. Jennie said, 'I don't want him to go to the bar, I want you to get up automatically like it's your job. Because you are your mother. Look at the way your father treats your mother and the way Isaac is treating you'. In the episode where Arthur and Dominic went to Clacton on Sea [17/50 'At First I Was Afraid' by Julia Gilbert], you saw my father get quite angry at times and my mother does things for him and goes very solemn, and Jennie said that it was just being echoed in the way Isaac was with me, and that's why Carole could see it straight off, but she couldn't tell me because I wouldn't believe her. Sometimes a director will give you a note that unlocks something for you, and as soon as she said it I went, 'Of course! Why hadn't I seen that?'"

One of the things I always like about David's acting that came out strongly in this storyline was his ability to show how that Dominic is putting on a public face, but might have different emotions going on underneath.

"Since I was a kid, watching anything, what hooks me emotionally is someone's eyes in a performance," he says. "It's why I love watching theatre when it's really close and you can see the expressions of the actors, as opposed to when you're sitting in the gods looking down and you can only really hear it. The eyes are where a lot of emotion comes from, whether you want it to or not. I learned that with Dom that's his give-away. He can be looking one way, but you'll see in his eyes what he's thinking. So I try to do that as subtly as I can do. You've got to be able to feel that emotion, and if you can't feel it you can't show it. So I have to pull on my own past experiences—those moments of having to be excited for someone but bitterly disappointed inside.

"I just had a scene with Camilla where Zosia said she was leaving. It's always about showing two things at once, it's always about that bit underneath that makes you say, 'Oh look – his heart's breaking!', but within the scene he has to be upbeat for her and say he's really proud of her. I always look for that on TV or in theatre, or just talking to friends and stuff. There's always more than one thing going on and it's about being able to show those emotions at the same time because it gives a clearer emotional picture. In my head I see it as making it 3D. It's not just, 'I'm walking and picking up this file', it's, 'Why are you picking up that file? How should I pick it up? What mood am I in?' I could pick it up in a quick, angry way, or tentatively like I'm really thinking about something else. So it's constant layering. That's how I do it, I have to pull everything apart and layer it back together to be able to allow the scene to blossom in the way that I hope it does. That's what I've learned from being on this job. I've learned so much over these last four years. For me, one of the things that chokes me up is seeing someone's eyes glass up, it always gives me that little choke moment. Camilla's great at doing that. She does a little thing with her breath as well, like a little intake of breath, and it makes you realise she's really struggling. You have to find these little tics for your character specifically. Dom's is the mask going on but you can see that behind it he's not coping, he's really sad or really angry."

David loves working with the other actors on Holby and feels like he's always learning from them. Straight after he talked to me he was due to film a scene with Guy Henry in Hanssen's office. "In between scenes he's making jokes, he's dancing around, doing silly voices, singing songs. And then he'll go straight into it and he'll nail the scene and he's so phenomenally talented like that. You just think, 'How has he done that?' Then afterwards he'll be like, 'My tea. Where did I put my tea?' It's a masterclass. It's a wonderful thing to watch. He just drops all the clowning and looks you dead in the eyes, and because of his stature and who he is, all of a sudden you go from joking and laughing to suddenly feeling really intimidated, which just works so wonderfully for the character. It's perfect."

He has signed up to stay at Holby for another year and is looking forward to seeing Dominic's character develop. "I'm intrigued to push the character a little more. Dominic's just become a registrar on the show, so he's gone up a notch." He'd also changed his appearance a little bit, with a new beard and moustache that he'd grown on holiday. "I had a week in Mykonos with my partner, just after the Isaac storyline. It had been so emotionally heavy that I needed a break and I just didn't care about my appearance for a couple of weeks. I wondered if that could be a Dominic thing. He's a thirty-something gay man, he changes his hair as often as he changes his clothes. So I said to Kate [Hall], I think it's a lovely idea that he's finding an identity again. He had an identity he found with Arthur, which vanished. He had another identity with Isaac which was destroyed, and now he's finding something else. He's been going to the gym a lot, he's been trying to find a physicality to himself on the outside. He doesn't like what's been going on inside, so he's trying to change the outside. The hallmark of anyone who's unhappy with their physical being and unhappy with the emotions they've been going through is to make big sweeping changes. And the facial hair does mature him as well, it adds a difference to him and he needed to come back different after all that. Obviously most of the time people see me in scrubs, there's not a lot I can change, but I can adjust bits like that. I think it just kind of worked. I Instagrammed it and got mass approval, though a woman did tweet me saying, 'Shave that thing off'."

He was also hoping that Dominic would have the chance to move around the hospital and work with other people. "Keller will always be his home, but there's a chance to go and explore a little bit. With the storylines coming up there's going to be opportunities to spend some time on different wards with different people. There are clearly three separate groups on the show and when they intermingle it creates a different dynamic for that episode. I've only done a couple of bits on AAU. I've rarely been to Darwin. The last time I was on AAU I did an episode with Jules Knight, so that was going back three years or so now. It's great for us to have a change of scenery and mix things up a little bit. I have the most amazing time working with Bob [Barrett] and we have great chemistry and the Sacha/Dom relationship works so beautifully, but it would be nice to see Dom working with someone like Jac. That would be interesting—a mixture of two very powerful personalities. With all the Zosia stuff I've recently been working with James Anderson and the Ollie/Dom dynamic is quite a funny, strange one. I think Dom sees him as sort of an embarrassing older brother! He likes him, but he thinks he's not cool, so he quietly mocks him. It's lovely to have the chance to work those dynamics out."

In the summer of 2017 viewers started to see an attraction develop between Dominic and Lofty (played by Lee Mead). "I think Dominic and Lofty is going to be a little bit Ross and Rachel in *Friends*," David says. "It's a very beautiful little dynamic which is being very carefully crafted at the moment. Lofty's come here and we learned very quickly that he's been in love with another guy. His sexuality was never really discussed in *Casualty*, so it was something we were open to do. I think Dom sees a lot of Arthur in Lofty's clumsiness and occasional ineptitude. He enjoys having someone like that around. Dom's had a few really dodgy relationships now and he's met somebody who's a very pure person, he's a good person with a good heart. He doesn't like messing people around and he doesn't play games. That for Dom is just the antidote, it's the balm on the sore of the relationships of his past. So at the moment they're both a bit unsure as to whether it's anything. They've been writing it very brilliantly, just keeping the audience not sure which way it'll go. There have been some lovely moments, at the wedding as well, some big moments there. It's been great for Dom to have that happiness. So many people are rooting for him to find happiness. But that's the problem, there's not enough drama in happiness so you have to keep people on their toes. People always want the characters to be happy, but when you've got fifty-two episodes a year you've got to keep it fiery, you can't just have fifty-two blissful hours. It just wouldn't work. It needs to be engaging and emotionally challenging for all of us."

JAMES ANDERSON (OLIVER VALENTINE)

People come up to me and say, 'Are you in Casualty?'
– *James Anderson*

James Anderson in person is not like Oliver Valentine at all. He looks like him, from the Darwin scrubs to the blue eyes, but James comes across as more reserved and thoughtful. Even his body language is slightly different. He's like Oliver Valentine's more serious, more modest, identical twin brother.

He admits he is self-conscious about watching himself on TV, even after many years of being an actor. "I find it difficult watching myself in anything, really," he says. "It takes a while to get used to. I used to hate it. I used to be unable to watch anything. It's okay now—you sort of distance yourself from your on-screen self. When I first started I would watch the playback—after the scene or the shot sometimes the director will review the take, and I used to do it because I was younger and a lot less experienced on screen. I would watch it to try and learn why you have to stand this way or look this way or whatever it is, because you are playing to a camera. I try not to now, because I find it makes me more self-conscious. It's like a mirror being on set and you find yourself looking at it and behaving differently. It's sometimes not very helpful."

He says that the most challenging thing for him as an actor in the high-pressure world of Holby was learning to manage his energy through the long days of filming. "You have to be able to concentrate completely on whatever it is you're doing at the required moment. You can't be completely in the zone from seven in the morning to seven at night and I found that hard when I first started. The day would end and I would just collapse, it was so exhausting because it's twelve hours of work that we do here. I wasn't used to that level of concentration, so I was on it all day, like a rabbit in the headlights. You can kind of see that in the performance as well and it kind of worked initially because I was an F1 and they are a bit rabbit in the headlights, they're inexperienced and green and in an environment that's foreign to them. So I used all of those things as an actor. I was surrounded by all these incredible people, some of them very famous and successful, most of them very experienced actors, and I was definitely one of the least experienced. There was me and Emma [Catherwood], who was my sister Penny, and we used that, I think. As F1s we had to feel that everyone around us knew better, and so defer to them. That's how I felt as an actor at that time as well, so it was quite easy in some ways.

"As a young actor it's sink or swim here. It's a lovely place to work but you have to go with it. It's got a kind of steamrollery feel to it—if you get in the way it's going to knock you down, so you just have to get on the steamroller and go with it. It's all about confidence, knowing that you are here for a reason and that's very special and it's yours, and you have to own that. For me, confidence is a huge part of what we do."

One of the things that I've always loved about Oliver Valentine is the comedy. He's often the one that comes out with witty lines, and I like the way he plays up his very British, reserved persona. That's also an aspect that James enjoys. "I love the comedy. There's quite a lot of physical comedy from time to time and I like that too. Ollie and I are similar in some ways, but very different in others. He has an innate confidence and things come easy to him and I don't have that, so I've quite enjoyed playing someone like that. It's water off a duck's back with Ollie quite a lot, but at the same time, when he fails it's quite enjoyable. When he struggles is when it's fun, because he doesn't see it coming ever and that's where the comedy comes. He has to work alongside some pretty forceful people—mostly Jac I suppose, but others too. It's when he comes up against them and doesn't see what they see, there is room for comedy. I try and play it straight. There are some one-liners, but Jac's are always better. It's quite annoying. I know the way it's built is: I'll get my little dagger in, but I'll end up losing in the end and get a withering look! But Rosie and I have fun with that as actors, seeing how I can really wind her up so in return she can devastate me."

James enjoys getting his teeth into the really dramatic stuff that Ollie has been given over the years, even at times when it was reflecting things going on in his own life. "I think the thing that cracked Ollie as a character was, sadly, his sister dying," he says. "You were given a dimension to his character that up to that point hadn't been seen and he hadn't experienced. He was young and to go through a bereavement at that age was really hard for him and he struggled, and to work on it as an actor was a real challenge for me. So that was the first big thing and his wife Tara died soon afterwards, which was not ideal. So those stories I really enjoyed. They were really hard work but very satisfying looking back on them.

"At the time my dad was very ill with cancer and he died around the same time I was working on the story of Penny's death. It was incredibly difficult and sad on one level, the obvious level, but I had my dad's love and support. He was so proud that I was in this show and he came here and visited the set. He wasn't an actor so he had no real understanding of what it was that I did, so I was able to show him that before he died and that was really great for me. I was also able to really invest in this story and know that there was something positive in doing it that felt redemptive for me, even though it was very sad.

"I explored that again with the Tara storyline. That was a year-long storyline that we always knew would end that way. She was brought into the show kind of to die, which is a bit bleak. For me, it's not therapy at all and I disagree with the idea of acting as therapy very much actually, but it's an outlet. If you've experienced something and you're able to put something of yourself into your work it's always the way to go, because then your acting is based on truth and reality. I've always enjoyed performances where you can see the actor is working with a line of truth. Even if they're playing killers or drug dealers, they can identify with something in those people that they carry in themselves. So for me it was obvious for a couple of years that I was able to use something sad, and working with fiction it was a positive thing for me."

After the Tara storyline James took a break to pursue other projects. He wasn't intending to come back, but when Oliver Kent and Simon Harper asked him if he would be interested in returning, he eventually said yes. "It's a place that I love, full of people I love, and they were offering me a really good story." The thing that interested him was that the eighteen-month break gave him and the writers a chance to reboot the character. "I came in as a slightly different version of Ollie, which I loved. It required me leaving to be able to take some of the boyishness out of the character—he's older, greyer, but more confident."

When we spoke, there were early plans for a big plot that would involve the whole hospital, and James had been told that Ollie might suffer a life-changing event. It was a prospect that he found both challenging and exciting, because it could be another opportunity to move Ollie forward as a character. "That could be something really meaty. The idea that he's going to have this injury that might potentially change him in some way, or he'll be fighting with what he used to be and trying to get back to that, but knowing he can't. It sounds terrifying to play authentically, so I'd want to really work hard on it beforehand. I think being terrified about it is a good sign because it means I care and I want to do it justice. When you stop being scared it's because you're being safe, which is lovely in some ways, but to be scared you're engaged and it's an indicator you're tuned in."

Holby fans always want to know whether the actors are squeamish, and James admits he is, in real life anyway. "I'm not squeamish here, because I know it's not real. The hearts we use, when you squeeze them they're like stress balls, it's quite fun, and they're all lubed up with oil to make them look shiny and lovely and washing up liquid to make it fit together neatly, and the blood is sugar syrup. You wear latex gloves and you get to fiddle around in these cavities. It's quite fun, it's like playing with those squidgy putty things. That's how I have to think of it.

If I thought of it as real, I think I'd pass out.

"When I started I went round a hospital and I was so over-sensitive and almost did pass out. I saw no blood. I was just trailing a doctor around on his ward rounds. Just going up to a bed, I was just so overwhelmed that this person in the bed was hanging on to every word this doctor was saying because their lives depended on it. The doctor was quite calm and dealing with this case and going on to the next one, but it was so humbling. And I was wearing scrubs so people thought I was a doctor. I was very emotional and I left that day completely exhausted, that sense of being on it for the entire shift was absolutely exhausting. I was very humbled and very emotionally drained. There was no blood or anything, but there was quite a lot to take in, definitely."

James loves the way Holby tells stories that affect the whole hospital. "It may be one event that affects one person, but the hospital moves around that story and we do it so well. The one I remember was when Luke [Roberts, Joseph Byrne] got shot and Daisha Anderson got shot away from the hospital [12/22 and 12/23 'The Butterfly Effect Part 1 and 2' by Justin Young]. The first episode was the fallout of this shooting and the second episode was the shooting itself. So it played with time firstly, which was weird and kind of wonderful. And secondly every single person here, all sixteen of the cast, was involved in the story. There was a comedic story going on and this very dramatic thing, and it was hearts and minds stuff, it was brilliant. For me, that is what Holby is all about. It's not about stars or main characters, it's an ensemble. Very much the whole building feels that way to me and it's really important that it stays that way. That's why I'm here, to tell my story in among a cohort of brilliant people—both on and off screen."

A lot of Ollie's storylines since he returned have been about his relationship with Zosia March (Camilla Arfwedson). "I've worked with Camilla a lot over the last three years. As a working relationship we've really enjoyed having each other to play off. It's been a long arc of a story, and we've enjoyed working on stuff that isn't necessarily all on the page and trying to mine the story for stuff that's beyond a rom com or stuff that we're given. I think that's testament to her and I have really enjoyed working with her."

We met while the run-up to Ollie and Zosia's wedding was being filmed, and in real life James had got engaged himself a few months previously and was planning his own wedding. "I honestly think they're following me around and taking notes," he laughed. "It's a bit weird. Everything I seem to do here is like an echo of my own life. Our real wedding is the same week as my wedding here goes out on screen. Hopefully we'll have a happier ending than Ollie does." He said he and his fiancée both liked the idea of having children. "It would be very nice. I'd like to be a dad. I'm quite broody. I think Ollie wants to be a dad too!"

I said that Ollie had nearly managed it with Chrissie Williams shortly after James joined the show. In fact, Ollie was initially quite the ladies' man. "Obviously the writers had gone away and written three or four months of Oliver Valentine before me having been cast," he says, "so he was written as this real alpha, a real Lothario. And he arrived and started shagging all these nurses and doctors and whatever around the hospital, but that's not something that I could tap into very easily, so I was kind of playing against that lover boy character." He says that characters often evolve as the writers see what the actor is like in the role. "The writers don't really have a sense of who you are until they've seen you, and that only happens a couple of months in. So you'll see when Rosie initially played Jac, the character changes quite a lot once she inhabits the character. The same happens with every character, you find your way with the initial brief and inhabit it in your own way. If it works it's really exciting and the writers can go away and know who this person is now, and then you can get momentum on the character."

He says the actors feel ownership of their characters "and it's weirdly private for us". He likes the challenge of saying the words that are in the script, and feels that's his job, but he will finesse a line slightly if he thinks that would make it more like Ollie. "I quite like to ad lib sometimes, just add bits and pieces to lift it a little bit. If you're invested in the scene, a little bit here and there will be authentic. Those moments will often make it to the screen because they're truthful moments that come out of playing the truth of that scene. To get to that bit where you're able to ad lib, you're not trying to show off, it's coming from telling the story, so it feels right. If it doesn't feel right I wouldn't bother."

He says he enjoys the process of rehearsal, but there's very little time to do that at Holby. "I love the rehearsal period because that's where you're playing and teasing out what's going on. I love that. When you commit it to camera it's almost like you're giving it away and it's someone else's problem—editors etcetera. That's why watching your own work back can feel disappointing in some ways, because your bit of the process is the creating of it. After that it doesn't belong to you any more, someone else can scrutinise it, say you don't look a certain way, pick what they like and don't like."

In the past James has directed a short film ("I was in it but we cut me out") and really enjoyed the experience. "I love watching actors work and seeing the choices they make. And I love visual storytelling," he says. He would like to direct again, but doesn't think he'd follow in Hugh Quarshie's footsteps by directing an episode of Holby. "To go from being an actor, I would imagine the crew would look at you differently, other directors would think of you differently, it's redefining who you are. If I did do it here I wouldn't want to be in the episode. I'd need to just completely distance myself and come in cold from a different angle."

James lives in London and doesn't often get approached in the street by fans ("I don't have an interesting day-to-day life"), but he says outside of London it is quite noticeable. "I do tweet but I'm not that good on it and I use it to look at what's going on in the world kind of thing. So I'm not really aware of my profile I suppose, so when it does happen it's quite strange. I enjoy it when I'm with my friends because they think it's ridiculous when people come up to me and say, 'Are you in *Casualty?*', which is invariably what they say. My friends love that."

Usually the reaction he gets is very favourable. "People didn't like it when Ollie cheated in his exams, I had some aggro from people, but generally it's really positive," he says. "I enjoy that the show is a loved show and the people who watch it aren't haters. It's lovely to have that attention because it's coming from people being supportive of the show saying they love it."

CAMILLA ARFWEDSON (ZOSIA MARCH)

I think her lifelong affair will be her work, her brain
and her ambition. – *Camilla Arfwedson*

I met Camilla at the end of May 2017 and she was due to leave in July. "It was my decision," she told me, and said she had a mixture of feelings about going. "I've been here a long time and been given amazing storylines, my bipolar storyline and my storyline with my dad and my storyline with James [Anderson, Ollie Valentine]. And my storyline with the boys, David [Ames, Dominic Copeland] and Rob [Ostlere, Arthur Digby]. I feel like Zosia has reached a peak, reached happiness with meeting Ollie and has dealt with everything in her life, so it felt like it would be a good time to take a break really. Maybe do some other things.

"There are moments when I feel quite sad about it, because it's been such an amazing place for me and for this character to grow in, and I've had a lot of fun and made a lot of friends. The atmosphere is amazing here, that can never be underestimated. There are days like today when I've been messing around with David on set downstairs and we just laugh and laugh and laugh and do some really good work at the same time and you think days like this are just golden. So I'm going to miss that. But then I'm really excited about doing something new. My agent has wanted

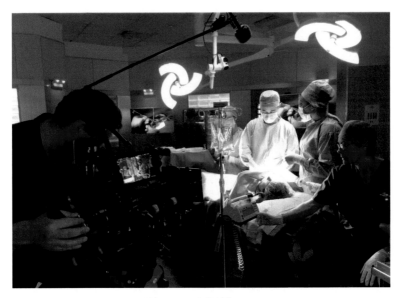

Filming in AAU Theatre

Bob Barrett and Rosie Marcel

Filming the green screen
sequence for 19/27

Filming in Darwin Theatre

David Ames and Bob Barrett

David Ames and Camilla Arfwedson film an emotional scene
for 19/11 ('The Nightmare Before Christmas' by Katie Douglas)

The Wyvern entrance to the hospital

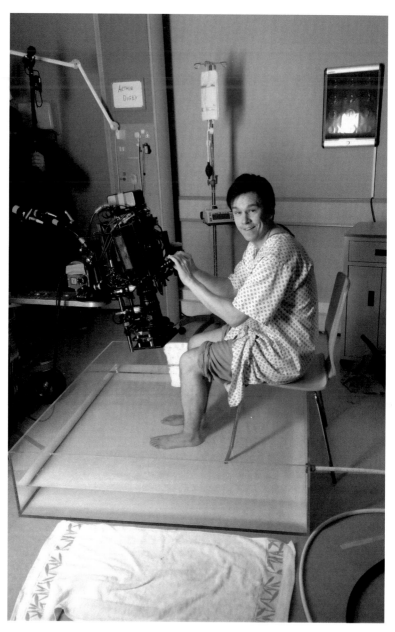

Filming Arthur's wet feet for 18/35 ('I'll Walk You Home' by Andy Bayliss)

Rosie Marcel through the lens

Jemma Redgrave and Catherine Russell having a Berena moment

Kaye Wragg and Joe McFadden filming in the AAU Victorian corridor

Kaye Wragg and Joe McFadden talk to director Paulette Randall

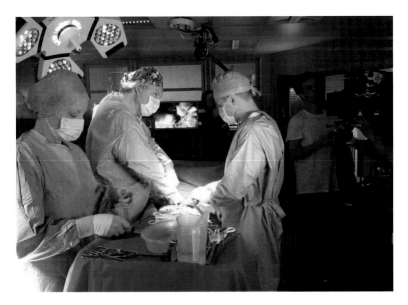

Filming in Keller Theatre

Marc Elliott and David Ames

Dominic's injuries from his fall in 19/27

Guy Henry sporting traditional
Swedish wedding attire for 19/13

Another view of L-shaped
Neptune House

The Garden

Men in black: (L–R) Alex Walkinshaw, Christian Vit, Guy Henry and David Ajao

Bob Barrett shows off Sacha's new look for 19/7 ('The Kill List' by Jeff Povey)

Jac and Sacha have a private moment in the garden

'Video village' – the view the camera is capturing for 19/27 ('Someone to Look After Me' by Patrick Homes) watched by the script supervisor (L) and the director (R)

Pulses – and the cupboard that isn't a cupboard

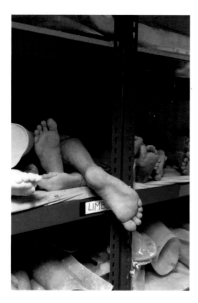

Chamber of horrors, also known as
the prosthetics department

Making an ulcerated leg in the
prosthetics department

The 'view' from Hanssen's office window

WYVERN ENTRANCE, KELLER AND DARWIN

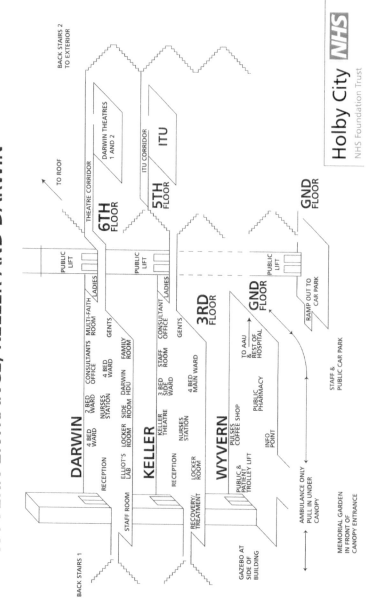

DARWIN

BACK STAIRS 1

RECEPTION | STAFF ROOM | ELLIOT'S LAB | 4 BED WARD | LOCKER ROOM | 2 BED WARD | NURSES STATION | SIDE ROOM | DARWIN HDU | CONSULTANTS OFFICE | 4 BED WARD | FAMILY ROOM | MULTI-FAITH ROOM | LADIES | GENTS

THEATRE CORRIDOR

6TH FLOOR

DARWIN THEATRES 1 AND 2

TO ROOF

BACK STAIRS 2 TO EXTERIOR

PUBLIC LIFT

KELLER

RECEPTION | KELLER THEATRE | NURSES STATION | 3 BED SIDE WARD | 4 BED MAIN WARD | STAFF ROOM | CONSULTANT OFFICE | LADIES | GENTS

ITU CORRIDOR

5TH FLOOR

ITU

PUBLIC LIFT

WYVERN

RECOVERY TREATMENT | LOCKER ROOM | PUBLIC & PATIENT TROLLEY LIFT | PULSES COFFEE SHOP | INFO POINT | PUBLIC PHARMACY | TO AAU & REST OF HOSPITAL

3RD FLOOR

GAZEBO AT SIDE OF BUILDING

AMBULANCE ONLY PULL IN UNDER CANOPY

MEMORIAL GARDEN IN FRONT OF CANOPY ENTRANCE

GND FLOOR

STAFF & PUBLIC CAR PARK

RAMP OUT TO CAR PARK

GND FLOOR

PUBLIC LIFT

AAU BLOCK

GROUND/MEZZANINE

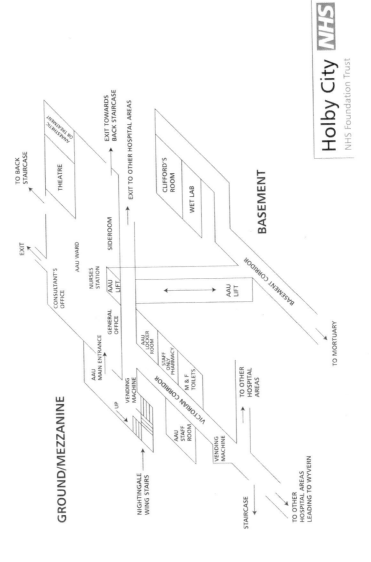

NIGHTINGALE WING STAIRS

UP

VENDING MACHINE

AAU MAIN ENTRANCE

CONSULTANT'S OFFICE

EXIT

AAU WARD

NURSES STATION

GENERAL OFFICE

AAU STAFF ROOM

VICTORIAN CORRIDOR

AAU LOCKER ROOM

STAFF ONLY PHARMACY

M & F TOILETS

VENDING MACHINE

TO OTHER HOSPITAL AREAS

STAIRCASE

TO OTHER HOSPITAL AREAS LEADING TO WYVERN

SIDEROOM

AAU LIFT

TO BACK STAIRCASE

THEATRE

ANAESTHETIC OR TREATMENT

EXIT TOWARDS BACK STAIRCASE

EXIT TO OTHER HOSPITAL AREAS

BASEMENT

CLIFFORD'S ROOM

WET LAB

BASEMENT CORRIDOR

AAU LIFT

TO MORTUARY

Holby City NHS

NHS Foundation Trust

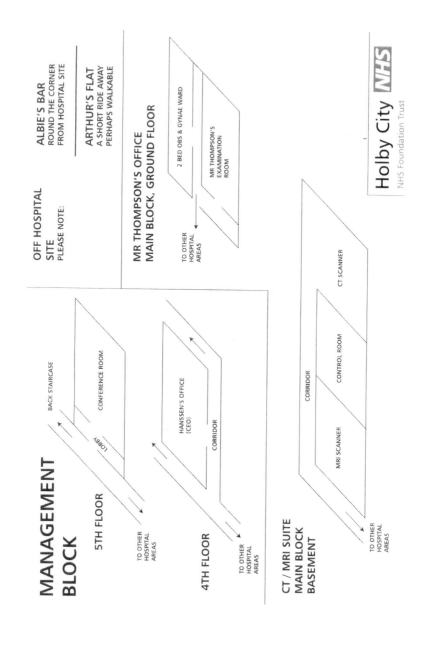

MANAGEMENT BLOCK

5TH FLOOR

BACK STAIRCASE

LOBBY

CONFERENCE ROOM

TO OTHER HOSPITAL AREAS

4TH FLOOR

HANSSEN'S OFFICE (CEO)

CORRIDOR

TO OTHER HOSPITAL AREAS

CT / MRI SUITE MAIN BLOCK BASEMENT

CORRIDOR

MRI SCANNER

CONTROL ROOM

CT SCANNER

TO OTHER HOSPITAL AREAS

OFF HOSPITAL SITE
PLEASE NOTE:

ALBIE'S BAR
ROUND THE CORNER FROM HOSPITAL SITE

ARTHUR'S FLAT
A SHORT RIDE AWAY PERHAPS WALKABLE

MR THOMPSON'S OFFICE
MAIN BLOCK, GROUND FLOOR

2 BED OBS & GYNAE WARD

MR THOMPSON'S EXAMINATION ROOM

TO OTHER HOSPITAL AREAS

Holby City NHS
NHS Foundation Trust

me to go off and do something new for quite a while, try other things, go to America. I've got a manager in America, so we'll try and see if we can get anything out there."

There were no plans to kill off the character of Zosia, so the door would be left open for Camilla to return at some point. "If I can come back, that would be amazing too, because like I say it is such an amazing place to work. So I'm excited! I'm nervous, because nothing might happen and I'm not arrogant enough to think I'm going to jump into another job, I'll have to hustle a little bit like I did before. The big wide world is quite a scary one, so we'll see."

I told her I thought there was more that could be explored with Zosia's character and she said she hoped the rest of the Holby audience would think so too. She has some ideas herself. "I'd quite like to see her *not* in a relationship," she says. "I don't want her to become like Jac, because that would be too obvious. I think you can be a feminist but not be a man-hater. I feel like Zosia's happiness has revolved around her finding this perfect young man in Ollie, and building a home with him and becoming happy and being in love and having a romantic idyll with him, getting married. She hasn't really been true to herself and I don't think she really is a person who's going to end up being married with two children. I wonder if she might want to travel the world. She's much more ambitious than she's allowing herself to even think about at the moment because she wants to have this perfect relationship. She probably thought for a long time that she couldn't have a relationship because she was so messed up. She probably did hate men quite a lot because of her relationship with her father, didn't trust men particularly, probably didn't have enough confidence and security within herself to think she can love someone else, because she doesn't love herself. So she's done all that and she's projected all that on to Ollie and I think that's why the marriage doesn't work out.

"I think her lifelong affair will be her work, her brain and her ambition. Like her dad, Guy Self, really. I think she's quite similar to her dad. Hopefully not as ruthless as him, but she's definitely got that side to her. I think she's quite tough."

In discussions about the character with series producer Kate Hall,

Camilla had said she would love it if Zosia got married on a beach in ten years' time when she's in her forties, and maybe adopted a child. "Kate said, 'Exactly. Why don't we make her that kind of modern woman?'" Camilla says. "Happiness is so often depicted as you're being paired off with someone, and you don't have to necessarily be paired up with anyone. Work can be your love, where you live can be your love, travelling can be your love, your family can be your love, your friends can be your love, you could have pets who could be your love. You never know. You build your own world and it doesn't have to be about a man. So that's what she's doing in this series, she's going, 'I don't want to have my father in my life, I don't want to have to be responsible for him and I don't really want to be in this relationship with Ollie. I'm going to go off and do my own thing.' And maybe one day come back and explore other things. That would be great. But as a slightly different, more grown-up woman. I think she needs to leave in order to come back and explore that."

I told her that both James Anderson and Jaye Jacobs said that when they came back after being away from Holby for a while, they both thought that their characters felt fresh and like there were new things about them to explore. "You'll come to the character with so many per-spectives won't you?" Camilla said. "Hopefully my life will then inform Zosia when she comes back, and seeing Zosia as an older woman will be interesting. I think she's the kind of person who could become quite senior here. She's got that tenacity and that character. I think that's what they were probably aiming for when they first wrote her. They wanted her to be a little bit similar to Jac. She's not a soft little flower, is she? She's troubled and she's very capable and sometimes that makes for a very good leading character in a place of high pressure like this."

A big reason why Camilla was going to find it hard to leave was the friendships she'd formed at Holby. "It was so fun working with Rob and David. The chemistry between us has gone beyond the screen and we're all really good friends in real life. We're always in touch with each other, we always go out together, we plan weekends away and we just laugh and laugh and laugh. It's just the most amazing casting to put us three together. You'd never have imagined it would work. When we first met each other we were a bit wary of one another, and then we just ended up having so much fun. That obviously translated on screen and you could see the chemistry, and the audience responded really well to it. Three young professionals muddling their way through their private lives and their working lives together, and living together and going out together, and it was really great and felt really realistic and they wrote it really well. We found a lot of humour in it as we were playing it."

Of course that trio was broken up when Rob Ostlere left Holby in series 18. "It was so sad when Arthur [Digby] died," Camilla says. "It was really sad for all of us actually, it felt like a real blow in real life when Rob left, because he played it so brilliantly as well so it felt quite real." She looks emotional for a second and gives herself a little shake. "Ugh! So we all struggled a bit and I think we all got a bit depressed as a result for a few months. We were all really overwhelmed with it.

"I think this is what happens. When David was going through his abuse storyline he became very sensitive and retreated into a bit of a shell for a few months. And I definitely felt like I was going a bit crazy when I was doing my bipolar stuff. You start to take on the emotions of the character, because you're living it every single day, seven till seven, and you're reading it at home. It's very heavy storylines they've given us— cancer, domestic abuse and bipolar, so it's been quite full-on for all of us. But it's been amazing."

She told me she'd researched the bipolar storyline by reading a lot about it and watching TV documentaries. The medical researchers sent her a lot of information. She found playing the storyline very intense. "They cottoned on to the fact that I could play this storyline, so they really threw it at me, which was a real challenge. I really, really liked doing it. It's very hard to do when you're on such a fast schedule and you don't get the time to rehearse it.

"They let me get on with it and that was the best way of doing it. I thought, 'I'm going to play it the way I've practised it and the way I've read about it. I'm going to do it my way'. And they trusted me with it. So that was great because they put that faith in me, but the amount they threw at me was quite a lot, so there'd be days when it was just very full-on. Then I'd go home and read the scripts, which sometimes were coming quite late so you didn't have much time at all. That could be difficult. The speeches were really hard to learn. It's not exactly like Shakespeare or a normal monologue, because it doesn't make any sense. You jump from idea to idea to idea, so I had these crazy maps in my head I had to plan out. And I had an acting coach come and talk to me about mental illness and how to play it. That was really helpful because I had really big episodes where I completely lost it. I felt I really had to do it justice because it's a very serious topic. Lots of kids watch the show and lots of kids suffer from this and they do not understand what they're going through, their parents might not know what they have, they haven't been diagnosed yet. Then they see this girl on TV and they think, 'That's what I have – I have these episodes'.

"We had a lot of people writing in and getting very attached to Zosia when she was at her most vulnerable. It was probably because she seemed so strong and capable and suddenly there was this other complete flip side to it. It felt like I had a responsibility to them and to anyone who has this kind of medical condition because it's very serious and very troubling. It's horrific, really, and having lived through it as my character I can only give them my biggest sympathy, because it sounds like you're living in hell when it happens.

"The acting coach helped me make much more sense of how to play it. The key thing was that when you're playing this character who's mentally unwell, everything makes complete sense to her. So when she was having these manic episodes and plucking things from thin air, it made complete sense to her. And that's what made it sadder to watch. To her everything seemed logical and she didn't know why no one was understanding her."

We talked about the episode where Digby died and you can read about Camilla's thoughts on the emotional scene when Zosia broke down in Jac Naylor's arms, in that chapter. And then she was called away by the director to rehearse the last scene of the day. "I don't know it! I need to go and learn it. I thought I had a scene off!" she said, and dashed away.

BOB BARRETT (SACHA LEVY)

There's something about Holby, it has a lightness and
a smile and a warmth, and I think that's down to
how well we all get on. – *Bob Barrett*

I'd met Bob Barrett a couple of times at Holby before I interviewed him, and on each occasion he gave me a great big hug. He really is every bit as lovely as you'd expect from his portrayal of Sacha. The staff in the fifth-floor office told me they joke about Bob having a *Dorian Gray*-type picture in his attic at home of Grumpy Bob, because they always see him smiling and laid-back.

His personality obviously suits the character he plays. "When I started I was told that Sacha was going to be the best friend to everyone in the hospital. Initially I floated between AAU and Keller and had contact with so many people, and that really worked for Sacha as a character I think."

Sacha was originally seen in the show in series 12 as the father of Chrissie Williams's baby after a one night stand. "When I first came I was very lucky because I hadn't seen the show really, so I did the first couple of episodes then there was a big gap of two months before I came back so I blanket-watched every episode I could find of Holby," Bob remembers. "I saw where I fitted and why I was picked, because what they needed was someone with a smile on his face who's a nice guy. So I knew when

I came in that that was where I'd fit in, I guess. There are a lot of characters on the show who are alphas—Guy Self, Matteo Rossini, John Gaskell, Ric Griffin, Michael Spence. And Oliver Valentine is becoming more of an alpha, in a very interesting way. Sacha has a quiet authority which comes from being the best doctor he can be. He's got a terrible temper, which I love, but there will always be an apology or a forgiveness."

Bob loves his current Keller family of Kaye Wragg, David Ames and Lee Mead. "We get on stupidly well, it's brilliant. Lots of people say they love coming to Keller because we do have so much fun. Lee is a really good addition to it. We always say people come and go but there's the three of us: me, David and Kaye, and people come in and out of that. Lee fits in so well that the three musketeers have become the four musketeers almost. I love my stuff with Kaye and I love working with her and who knows where that will go, but a bit like my relationship with Jac, it's important that it's always there and always special, in whatever shape or form it's in. And I feel that with David. The stuff that's happened with me and David has happened quite organically. I love my stuff with David. We've got a great relationship. It's great, but over the years I've worked with so many people. I'm on Keller pretty much full time now. I think the idea is they're going to float lots of people around the different wards, but I don't think they're going to float me or Rosie, because I'm Mr Keller and she's Ms Darwin. I'd love to work with James [Anderson] more, though. I had loads of scenes with James when I started and I never see him now."

Different aspects to Sacha's character have more recently been seen, with his depression storyline and the storyline about him reconnecting with his Jewish faith. "With every character who's here for a long time you should see more and more layers of who they are," Bob says. "The classic case is Jac. Over the years you've seen her peel back the layers, and that's what I want to do now with Sacha, show more and more of what goes on underneath. The nice thing about the depression storyline is that it wasn't public—only Essie and Jac knew about it. Usually when something happens in the hospital everyone knows about it."

I said that it had perhaps been a bit too low-key for some viewers, who thought that the story came and went in the space of one episode

(19/29 'Two Hearts' by Katie Douglas). "I liked the quietness of the storyline" Bob says. "It all stemmed from his break with Essie [in 18/48 'Brave New World' by Katie Douglas] and it made complete sense that that would happen because of the nature of the split. I remember watching the episode back where we split and watching Sacha, and even as me doing it I sort of worried for him because he didn't look right at the end of that episode. But the storyline started off all bright and funny with him dyeing his hair and the motorcycle, and then it got worse and worse. I did research on depression and a lot of people said it takes you by surprise, and some days you're fine and other days it just whacks you between the eyeballs. What was clever about the storyline was you had that episode where he had had liposuction and at the end of that you thought he was in a bad way. Then the Dom and Isaac stuff happened and he was involved in all that. Sacha's very good at hiding and covering what's going on underneath by caring for other people, so he shelves how he feels because he's not an ego and he hides it all. It was very in keeping with the way I see him. He doesn't want to bother people and he thinks he can sort it out himself. And of course he can't. So if the storyline had shown this going on for months, with him stealing stuff and you'd seen all that build-up, in a way it's more real the way it's been done. I remember the episode after the big breakdown, he seemed fine. He goes for his shvitz and he's fine. I talk to people who have depression and they say it's very accurate because what happens is you are fine and you think it's fine and then it comes back. I hope we'll see it coming back in a different form. You don't expect depression to happen when you're fifty-one, so I think it's interesting. The single most important thing for me was to make it as real as possible, so his storylines are played out over the right period of time to make him as real and as human as possible. It seems to me that's Sacha's role in the show, apart from being the one who's positive and keeps everyone going. They keep describing him as the healer, the guy that fixes people, that's his raison d'etre. He is fallible. There are a lot of people in the hospital who are superhuman, but he's just very real and human and flawed and tries his hardest."

Like Kaye Wragg, Bob firmly believes in the partnership of Essie and Sacha. "Essie is the one for him," he says. "She is his love, the One.

It won't stop him possibly having a relationship with someone else, but he feels however much it hurts to see her like that he can cope with it. He's very good at coping."

Aside from all this seriousness, there's a lot of comedy on Keller and I asked Bob how he managed not to laugh in the episode where Sacha dyed his hair (19/7 'The Kill List' by Jeff Povey). "I had that awful hairstyle the whole day," Bob said, laughing at the memory of it. "By the time we did that scene [where Sacha said, 'I look absolutely ridiculous, don't I?', and Dominic replied, 'Only from the scalp up. The rest of you is 100% to die for'] we still found it funny, but we weren't laughing as much. David and I really get on, so we laugh about other things. There was a scene I had with David, Rob [Ostlere] and Camilla [Arfwedson] in the bar and she had to do a Geordie accent, and the end of the scene was meant to be that and we just looked at her. At the end of the scene I improvised without telling them. So she did the accent and I went, 'Welsh, was it?' and they laughed spontaneously. And they kept it in. We do improvise a lot, though we didn't improvise in that hairstyle scene.

"I laugh every day, we all do. We were filming a scene the other day and Kaye was laughing so much they had to cut because her ears had gone pink. They must hate us! But to me that helps the show, because it has a smile. There's something about Holby, it has a lightness and a smile and a warmth, and I think that's down to how well we all get on. We're allowed leeway to be like that, and with the crew as well. We're on set for eleven hours, but the day just bounces along. I love it."

Something that audiences love is the relationship between Jac and Sacha. Bob agrees. "When I first started on Holby I worked with Rosie [Marcel] for six months, which was the best. That was Simon [Harper]'s idea, to put these two opposites together. The first day Rosie and I worked together they brought two scenes forward because we were working so quickly, we just flew. I thought it was great. Kate [Hall] was saying that in the focus groups they do, what comes up is that the most popular relationships are not the romantic ones, it's the friendships—Digby and Dominic, Jac and Sacha—that people adore. You look forward to those scenes because you know it's not going to be about bickering or about ripping clothes off and snogging in the bike sheds, it's about doing something that's going to make you laugh or warm your heart. I think that's very important. Rosie and I had this idea that while Sacha and Jac are single they should move in together as friends, like the odd couple, and live together in a flat. You won't see us in the flat, and she has ideas like she's horrible to someone, then I'm on the phone talking about what we're going to have for dinner that night."

Bob felt there were still a lot of stories about Sacha he wanted to tell. "Once an audience gets to feel like they know a character, that's when the interesting part comes and you can reveal more. He's a man who's all about family and relationships, and he's single and alone, hardly sees his kids and he's in his fifties, so it's like square one. He's not exactly moved on in his life at all in eight years. You think, what's happened to him in eight years? He's become a consultant and that's it. After a struggle! I looked at Arthur Digby and Elliot Hope and Sacha and Mr T, and they're quite similar types of characters, and I'm the only one left now doing that sort of thing. Characters that mean well, that have a lack of ego. They're not in it for themselves. Through whatever accident of personality they're unable and don't want to project themselves forward, which makes them very, very different doctors to other people in the show."

ELEANOR FANYINKA (MORVEN DIGBY)

It's like opening a present every single time
you get a script. – *Eleanor Fanyinka*

Although it was May when I had this conversation with Ellie Fanyinka, she was wearing a big fluffy brown dressing gown over her AAU scrubs. "I'm always cold!" she said. We settled down in a room that was a little bit warmer than AAU (but still had the wind howling at the fifth-floor window), and talked about the storylines that she was currently filming.

"Jasmine dies, and that's another huge hit for Morven, because Jasmine filled a little void for her," she says. "Not Arthur's void, but she was a really good, fun friend and she's very different to Morven so she brought out quite a different side to her. When she dies, it throws Morven in a very different way than Arthur's death did. I personally don't think that Morven has got over Arthur. I don't think she's even close to getting over it, it's all buried beneath work and lots of other stuff. I think she's repressed a lot of stuff. So when Jasmine dies it unpicks that scab and she feels lonely and thinks everybody leaves her, especially the people who are very close to her. I think we'll see some interesting sides of her character that we haven't seen before.

"I went up to the edit just now and watched one of the episodes where she's drinking. I don't know if they're going to run with it, but so far it's been a little bit of a thing. I don't think she sees it as anything that's wrong and she doesn't think she has a drink problem, but I think she's kidding herself a little bit. But we'll see."

Ellie told me that before she got the part she was working in a call centre where lots of actors work in between acting jobs. "I was sitting next to Rob Ostlere's best friend! I found out I'd got the part and Rob's best friend is sitting next to me and he asked who I was going to be on a ward with and I said, 'Arthur Digby, played by Rob Ostlere'. He took a picture of me and sent it to Rob, saying, 'I think this is going to be your new love interest'. A week later I went for a tea in Angel and I walked into this cafe and Rob is sat there and I'd never met him before in my life. So we sat and had coffee that day. Weird." She also said her brother is a massive Holby fan, and he once said to her, "'Ellie, there's this one actor on Holby, he's subtle, he's brilliant, he's a great actor. You should watch it sometime'. Of course he meant Rob, and when I got the part and said I'd be playing Rob's girlfriend, he said he'd obviously made that happen."

She really enjoyed her first day. "It was amazing, it was lovely. My first scene was on the stairs. It was a scene with Rob where I had an 'I want to succeed' type of speech. I was just excited. You learn your lines back to front so nothing can go wrong. The only thing I was afraid of was not hitting my mark and stuff like that. But the adrenaline's flowing, you're hyped up. So when I look back at the first episode [17/38 'Losing Control of the Wheel' by Julia Gilbert] I cringe! I feel like I'm doing so much. Having not done much telly before that and doing more theatre, the camera picks up a lot and maybe I didn't need to demonstrate stuff as much as I did. You don't have to do as much as you think you need to do.

"A lot of people hate watching their stuff. I watch everything because I want to improve, and there is such an art to being in front of a camera that I think you only learn when you are in front of a camera. I want to know where I'm going wrong. I can see why people hate watching themselves, because it's weird. It's difficult enough listening to your own voice. But for me, it's important. You can see what works and what doesn't and you can watch other people and learn so much.

"Watching Rosie [Marcel] and her stillness and her power is phenomenal. What's fascinating is that everyone has different ways of approaching the text. For instance Catherine [Russell] is a very dear friend of mine and last year when I was in between homes I lived with her for a month. She's so kind, I just love her. While I lived with her I watched her process and what she does with a script and she is so unbelievably thorough. She will go through the script with a fine-tooth comb. If something doesn't quite make sense, if something's wrong in the story, if she knows she said something ten episodes previously that contradicts what she's saying in this episode, she will know. I like to think I work hard on my script, but not to the same level that Catherine does. She works really hard.

"Then with Alex [Walkinshaw], his knowledge of the camera and where it is is phenomenal, he knows exactly how to make the shot work. Lucinda [Dryzek] is a completely organic actress, she's the sort of person who picks something up and she'll play with the scene in the moment. I think she doesn't go home like Catherine does and break down every single line, she will do it in that moment. She'll be on set and say, 'I'm just going to say it like this', and then she'll just fling the script aside and what comes on camera is magic. I don't know how she does it. To have the confidence to do that is incredible. So it's wonderful being able to pick up on everyone's different styles and take bits of it that work for me. And of course different scripts bring different things. Like with the Andy Bayliss script for [18/35] 'I'll Walk You Home,' I had to do a lot of work on that. It's not something I could have just rocked up on and just reeled off. Unfortunately I don't think I have the capacity to do that because I get tongue-tied and nervous and weird and my confidence drops through the floor, so I need to do work away from the set."

With experience she's found that she can learn scripts really quickly. "It's crazy how quickly I can learn a page now. Sometimes I can just read it through twice and I know it." Even the medical jargon? "Well that's always the same," she laughs. "FBCs, Us and Es, LFTs, group and save, they tend to be the same. Obviously if you've got something new and complicated it can really throw you. Sometimes you get a bit cocky and you think, 'I know that', and you'll turn up on set and you'll have to reel it off very quickly and it completely throws you, then you tell yourself you'll never be that cocky again. And you go home and you really, really work on the script for four months, then you think, 'It's okay, I've only got one line in this, it'll be fine', and that will be the line that throws you and they have to go through it again and again, and you're apologising to everybody for using up so much time. So you do need to do your work."

Working such long hours and learning lines in the evenings can mean that work can become all-encompassing, but Ellie revealed that she has ways to relax. "I get a little bit sad if I can't go to the gym, I find that really helps. I've joined the gym in Elstree as well so I try and go at lunch time sometimes, but that can be knackering if you're doing a full day and you're trying to find twenty minutes to eat as well. It's hard and you're on your feet all day. On a Friday a few times with Catherine [Russell] and Bob [Barrett] if we're getting the train home we will buy a little tinny from the newsagents and have a gin and tonic on the way home. I've done that with Rob [Ostlere] as well."

Ellie says that fans are generally lovely to her, although at the beginning the reaction to Morven wasn't always positive. "I remember people saying, 'Morven's so annoying', but I think that's subsided a little bit. I was so surprised, I didn't know how they could find her annoying. I think Lucy [Dryzek] found this as well. When you're coming into something and breaking up groups—like Morven was with Digby, Dom and Zosia—and threatening that dynamic, people go, 'Hang on a minute, we like things the way they are'. That's certainly happened with Jasmine and Oliver Valentine and the Zollie thing. People found that really hard to stomach. People don't like change, but we need change, otherwise it gets boring."

Ellie deals with this by reminding herself that the criticism is aimed at the character not at her. "Morven is not me. She's an element of me, because she's been imagined by me, but not just by me. Kate [Hall] and the story team created Morven, it was all their ideas. So they're not my words, they're Morven's. You can't take it too seriously. Saying that, she isn't a villain. I don't know about playing a villain, someone like Guy Self. I'm sure it goes over John Michie's head because he's suave and cool like that. So it doesn't get to me any more, but I don't go looking for it. If you do go looking for it you're going to find that for every five lovely comments there's going to be one person that says something not very nice. Everyone's entitled to their opinion. You're in their living rooms every week."

She loves the surprise of getting a new script. "It's like opening a present every single time you get a script because you think, 'What do they want me doing this time?' Like this whole thing around Jasmine's death and Morven drinking and sleeping with Damon. There's a scene I just watched where she's throwing up and she comes to work and she's really the worse for wear. That would never have happened when she first came, she was always on the top of her game, but now I think that's so exciting because people aren't one-dimensional. So throw more things at me, I say. I've had a lot of things recently where I square up to Jac Naylor, and people would say Morven is the person they'd least expect to do that, but my God she tries, and that's exciting. People do that in life a lot. She does have that inner fire."

GUY HENRY (HENRIK HANSSEN)

*I don't do muttering TV acting, I do stilted, stiff acting, so vocally
I suppose they thought we'd better make him Swedish. – Guy Henry*

It's quite unnerving when you see Henrik Hanssen loosen his tie, open the top button of his shirt and pop on a pair of sunglasses. I talked to Guy Henry in the sunshine in the Holby garden, just after the cast had all assembled outside the building for a group photo shoot, so all of the cast were in their character costumes. Guy says that Hanssen would *never* have his tie undone. "I rehearse like I am now with my shirt undone, the tie loosely tied. Then when we're about to go for a take I do my tie up, and I'm ready to go. So that's the moment when I begin to feel more like Mr Hanssen."

Guy is very fond of the character he plays. "Henrik Hanssen is a wonderful weirdo, I think. He's a very strange man. But I think people like the fact that he's tough but fair, he has a moral standpoint. When Guy Self was running the hospital I think people didn't like to see somebody in that position who didn't have an unwavering sense of doing what was right. It's a fanciful idea, but it's quite a nice one. For all his eccentricities and foibles I think Henrik is a man of principle, even if he's a bit odd at times. At least he does what he believes, he's not a devious politician

143

in that sense, though he is capable of manipulating things for his own ends. I don't think they're wrong things that he gets obsessed with—because he is obsessive, isn't he? Also he's got a twinkle in the eye. Behind the stiff, stilted, Swedish persona, he's actually quite funny. Some people I've met have said he's much nicer than he used to be, and we have to be a bit careful about that, we don't want to make him too bland and friendly and jolly. That would be wrong. He does have a sense of humour, though he pretends he doesn't. That's a joy to play, the twinkle. It's great fun to play whatever's going on underneath that slightly stern presence."

Ever since the storyline about Sahira Shah ended (14/27 'Ribbons' by Martha Hillier), I've always wondered exactly what Hanssen's feelings were towards her were. "He clearly had strong feelings for her as a person," Guy said. "He is very keen on championing people and supporting younger people. He's surprisingly good with children, we know that, he loves them. I think, rather sadly for him, when she said 'Are you in love with me Henrik?' and he went 'No! Get out,' I don't think he thought he was. I think he loved her and liked and admired her and was fascinated by her, but that's all he was capable of at that point."

He said he wouldn't like Hanssen to have a love story at the moment. "It's a double-edged sword. Either you maintain a distance from the character so he's an enigmatic, interesting, quirky, strange man that you never get to know really, or you open him up more than we already have. And that would be interesting too—it would be extraordinary, wouldn't it, for him to lose it? But I think on balance I would prefer to keep him out of a love story. It doesn't mean that he can't have passions and do interesting things.

"The Swedish episode where I went back and had a rapprochement with my dying father who I'd misunderstood [15/13 'Hanssen/ Hemingway' by Justin Young], I was in tears in that episode, so we know a bit about Hanssen. I think he finds life very difficult. He is a depressive and he finds day-to-day life hard. I think perhaps that's why people like him as well, because they can see that he's demanding and difficult and tough and a bit strange, but he tries to do the right thing, and he finds it difficult to deal with people on anything other than an official, professional level. But he manages. I love the fact that he doesn't care—he's not a snob, you see. There was an episode ages ago [15/4 'If Not For You' by Jamie Crichton] where he was having personal dark difficulties and finding life a bit tricky and he got talking in the bowels of the hospital to a Polish caretaker, played by a lovely actor called Robert Jezek. He was a great character and they wanted to keep him, but he'd signed a long contract in the West End in a musical. Hanssen loves talent, he likes people with drive and enthusiasm, but he doesn't care what rank they are in society, it doesn't interest him at all."

Guy says that when he auditioned for the role, the character was called Arnold Brown (though Simon Harper says the character was originally conceived as Middle Eastern and was called Akhbar). Guy is semi-serious when he says that they probably decided to make the character Swedish because of his performance. "When I joined in 2010 I'd never done a show like this before. I'd done lots of television and film and bits and bobs, and lots and lots of theatre. I think that's why they made him Swedish, because at my audition I was probably so stilted and theatrical that they thought, 'We'd like to have Guy Henry, but we think we'd better make him foreign'. On the page, the character was called Arnold Brown. Then, when they cast me, the next thing I knew I was Henrik Hanssen. And I'm sure it's because I've done so much Shakespeare. I don't do muttering TV acting, I do stilted, stiff acting, so vocally I suppose they thought we'd better make him Swedish." He smiles. "I might be making that up. I'm never quite sure why I'm Swedish, but by descent I am."

Simon Harper says that in fact it was Guy's height that made them think he could be Swedish. "We still wanted to keep the character of non-UK origin."

"It's always embarrassing when they keep putting in little bits of Swedish," Guy says. "Hopefully the smaller the better because it's not my finest hour I don't think."

He told me a funny story about an occasion when they tried to help him out with a Swedish dialect coach. "One day I had quite a big speech and we saw Hanssen rehearsing it in his office. They gave me a CD to listen to with how to say it, so driving to and from my home in south west London I was listening to it and trying to get it, because it's a very particular language. If they'd made him French or Spanish or something it might have been a little easier, because we know a bit about those, but Swedish is very foreign indeed. So I listened to this CD on the long commute and I thought I was getting very good at it.

"Then I came in on the day to film that actual scene and there was a total stranger, a lady, standing there in the corner, and she said, 'Oh no, no, no, you don't say it like that'. I said, 'Well I do, and I'm going to, because that's what I've learned'. And she told me how to pronounce a word, and I repeated it, and she corrected me, and it sounded exactly the same to me. Les—he's the grip who controls the camera moves and everything, very nice man, very funny—he decided that he knew exactly how this word should be pronounced and kept saying it his way, which was different again. As far as I'm aware, Les has never been any further north than Watford, so I don't know why, as a good Hertfordshire boy, he suddenly thinks he's an expert on Swedish. It was so funny."

A characteristic of Hanssen's dialogue is that he does tend to get long, elaborate lines. Guy says that this is an area where his theatrical background definitely helps. "I've spent years doing Shakespeare and Ben Jonson, Schiller, many of the classic theatre writers, and Restoration comedy, Sheridan. A famous, very frightening and now dead director at the National Theatre, Peter Wood, said, 'You start at the beginning of the sentence. You look round the Olivier Theatre as you're saying this long sentence, so you take all the audience in, then you finish your long sentence—all on one breath, it has to be all on one breath otherwise you'd better go home—and then you finish it in the middle of the Olivier so you can take all the audience in.' That's the Restoration Comedy style. You wouldn't do it for some other writers, but certainly to include the audience is a good thing."

When Guy arrived at Holby he was very confident in his stage-acting abilities, but less so about working in television. "I'm very grateful to Holby that you can't spend all day every day being frightened and neurotic about the fact that you don't like being so tall, you don't like your eyebrows, you don't like your teeth. At some point you have to give everyone a break and just get on with it and do it. Because otherwise you'd go under, and so would everyone else, if you spent all day being neurotic and tense and nervous about it, which I was to start with.

I had to make a decision pretty quickly to butch up and just do my best rather than be nervous and do less well than I should have done. I'm very grateful to Holby, because it's given me hours and hours and hours of experience in front of the camera.

"When I first came seven years ago I hadn't ever created a part that was totally new and they made no bones about it, it was an important new arrival," he says. "I was so frightened, it was terrifying. My first scene was with Amanda Mealing [Connie Beauchamp]. Apparently she said to Paul Bradley [Elliot Hope], 'He's all right, but he's very nervous.' I was! I was terrified. Sweating. It was 28 or 30 June 2010, in a very hot, grey wool suit standing in a very hot office sweating in front of Amanda Mealing, who was perfectly pleasant, but I was left under no illusion that it was an important character to get right. And it's been a great pleasure to develop him and play the character on and off for the last six years. It's been terrific. I love him. He's great. Funny man."

Henrik Hanssen is one of the most popular characters on *Holby City* and there are various online fan forums dedicated to him. Guy is a little bit bemused by all the attention. "I'm not on Facebook or Twitter," he says. "I do see some of the stuff. I have a friend who will sometimes show me the Facebook pages. I was flying to Belfast the other day. I'd been to a memorial service and I had far too much white wine and I was very jolly on the plane. It was only afterwards I saw someone had put a very lovely Facebook post up, saying 'I met his highness,' I think she called me, and saying I was such a gent. I was very glad, because I was as p****d as a fart! The photo looked quite jolly. When I meet people and they ask me for a photo I nearly always say yes, but I never know whether to be me, as in Guy, who's fairly smiley, or whether to be Hanssen-esque. I tend to veer towards the Hanssen-esque really, because that's who they know. I'm very fond of him and I'm very grateful to him and the whole Holby team for such a lovely part."

JAYE JACOBS (DONNA JACKSON)

The medical jargon I didn't remember at all. I couldn't even say
'Mr Hagenbach's laparoscopy'. – Jaye Jacobs

Donna Jackson was always one of my favourite Holby characters, so
when I heard she would be returning in 2017 after a six-year break, I was
really pleased. I met Jaye before her first episode as Donna 2.0 (19/38
'Paper Wishes' by Patrick Homes and Ailsa Macaulay) had aired. She
told me she was working with the Holby team to breathe life into Donna
once again. "We're trying to remember exactly who she is, because a lot
of people who are here now weren't here last time, so I might know more
about the character than they do. I always felt she was well-meaning, she
always came from a good place, though she sometimes got it wrong."

When we last saw Donna in 2011, she was going off to start a new
life in Liverpool with ex-soldier boyfriend Kieran and adopted daughter
Mia. Jaye told me that Donna returns to Holby without Kieran. "She just
alludes to it and says the relationship went south a long time ago. Then
a few episodes later on, she says, 'And in the end the nightmares came
back and he left us before he hurt us.'" Jaye looks emotional as she says
the line. "It killed me, that line, it kills me every time. It summed up
everything, that they still loved each other desperately and deeply, but

148

they couldn't be together, and it's really sad and makes me sad."

She laughs at how emotional the story is making her, and says returning to Holby has been emotional for her generally. "On the first day back, I met Kate [Hall] for the first time on set, and she said 'Jaye! Welcome home!' and I literally burst into floods of tears. It's very much a homecoming.

"I always hoped I would come back. I just left for personal reasons to have a bit of life experience, because I'd literally been here straight from drama school. I felt I needed to do other things if I wanted to be a full and complete person in my personal life. And also I want to bring some things to the part, and if all you've done is spend all your adult life in a BBC building there's going to be a limit to how much life experience you can bring. Holby had asked me to come back a few times, and my view was that there was nothing that I or Donna could bring to it. They were very kind and asked me again, and this time I realised there was something new to bring.

"While I was away I definitely thought about Donna as a naive twenty-something, thinking you just find the love of your life and that's it, the shoe always fits. When I was in my mid-twenties I was very happy to think of her in that situation. And then when I got to thirty and realised life didn't end at thirty, Donna became interesting to me again, because now she's a woman with life experience and that's way more interesting than a ditsy twenty year old who's just looking for a bunk-up or for love. So that's when I thought it could be time to come back because she was interesting again."

Jaye says that even though Donna is now older, she "never quite got her shit together, so she hasn't lost that element. She has a little more life experience, but essentially she's the same person." And Holby is a safe harbour for her. "I feel like Donna's been through her dark times and Holby's bringing her back into the light a little bit," Jaye says. "It's been a huge life saver for her. She's gone away and got it a bit wrong and it's just not working for her. Holby was there for her and I think this is her home. I'm just sad she's not with Kieran any more. When I was thinking about coming back, I thought, 'How will that work?', because I can't bear in my heart to think that Donna's not with Kieran any more, because it was such a perfect little ending."

Before she can get too emotional again we move on to talking about the medical jargon. Did it all come back to her easily? "I thought it would. It didn't you know!" she laughs. "I thought I would remember a lot more. Muscle memory kicked in and I knew how to put BP cuffs on and so on. But the medical jargon I didn't remember at all, it was really funny. I couldn't even say 'Mr Hagenbach's laparoscopy.'" She says it perfectly, then repeats it and mixes up laparoscopy and laughs. "See! Funny things catch you. I quite like the medical stuff, it's quite interesting."

She has her own approach to learning lines. "I'm quite systematic. I learn them and then sit and record other people's lines, so I can say mine in the gaps. Then I start saying them while I'm doing other things, like walking or making dinner. So you know the lines well enough that they can just trip out of you and you're not having to reach for them too much, and you can just get on with all the medical, physical stuff. Obviously, being a nurse, I get a lot of that to do, so it's easier if I've practised doing that. It has to seem like the medical stuff is something you do in your everyday life. 'Can you pass a scalpel, please? Can I have a pound of mince, please?' I think about it like that. I did have a rule about not learning lines in bed, because this permeates every aspect of my life and I need to have some time away from it, but at the moment I don't have that luxury because I just need to get them learned."

She's noticed some changes since she was last at Holby. "I started off when Darwin and Keller were one ward, and then we got the third floor and that became Keller. I feel like all my acting stuff was a lot different—lots of bed-making and hospital corners, lots of gloves, lots of taking bloods, all that. There's less of that now." Cast-wise, the only people she knows from before are Hugh Quarshie, James Anderson and Rosie Marcel, though she also worked with Alex Walkinshaw when they played a married couple on *Waterloo Road*. "I've always had really close friends on the show. It's weird to come in as the newcomer again," she says. "But everyone is so nice and welcoming. It's funny, I keep expecting certain people to rock up. Like Michael Spence, Hari [Dhillon], in his pencil suits. Those trousers were tight fitting, weren't they? Blimey! My eyes used to water just looking at those. But now we have the lovely Matteo [Rossini, Christian Vit] and his tight-fitting trousers." She grins, a totally Donna

Jackson grin. "I should probably stop or a law suit may ensue!"

Jaye says she hopes to stay at Holby for as long as Donna is still interesting to play. "It would feel awful if we still had this huge raft of stuff to explore to her. She's coming back to Holby as a mum of two. In my experience, when people have children they seem to relax into being nicer people."

I tell her it can't be too long before one or other of the children goes AWOL in the hospital corridors. "I've already shot that scene!" she says. "You're too big a fan!"

ROSIE MARCEL (JAC NAYLOR)

You can be clever and successful and a genius in surgery, and not report
to a man. And Jac doesn't really report to anybody. – *Rosie Marcel*

"I'm a bit scared to meet you," I tell Rosie Marcel as we sit down in
the green room on the fifth floor at Holby. Especially as she's wearing
Darwin scrubs and looks ready to do a spot of surgery and rip an F1s
head off before lunch.

"Everybody says that!" she says. "Everybody's always surprised that
I'm actually quite a nice person. Playing Jac for as long as I have has
certainly made me nicer—I just say the most awful things on set and
I feel so guilty afterwards. But no, I'm a lovely person." She says even the
crew are a bit scared of Jac. I tell her that when I was on the Darwin set
I was a bit shocked to see a member of the crew sitting in her chair, at
her desk, in her office. "Jac would have killed him," she says. "We use my
office to hang about in during filming, but weirdly no one usually sits in
my chair. I'll find out who that was and have him killed!"

Rosie says she loves the character she plays. "I wouldn't have still been
here after eleven years if I didn't enjoy the part, and they still manage to
find something to do with her, which I think is great. I still get the most
wonderful lines, which I love. She's a very funny soul, isn't she? She's not

a very nice person, but she's a person you love to hate. There's a little bit of her that everybody would like to have within themselves. She's that person you want to channel when someone's upset you or annoyed you and you want to say something quickly or sharp. She says all the things you say in your head that you wouldn't say out loud. She has no internal dialogue at all, and I think we all want to be a little bit more like that, more spirited. Hers just comes from lack of love and total self-preservation. That's who she is and I love that about her."

Rosie reveals an aspect to Jac that I'd never really thought about, but as soon as she says it, it seems obvious. "It's only ever the audience who get to see Jac really in her darkest points," she says. "It's only ever the audience or Sacha, nobody else ever sees her weaknesses and I love that, because it tends to give the audience a sense of control over that character and to feel like they get an exclusive look into her. I don't think that was deliberate at first. I think I once said to the producers, 'I don't know if you've noticed, but you never let anybody else see Jac's emotions apart from the audience, and if you've done it on purpose it's genius because it makes the audience feel like they get something exclusively for them'. And I think they jumped on that a little bit. And the audience loves the friendship with Sacha and again nobody else gets to see that friendship apart from them. If they've done it on purpose it's genius, and if they haven't it's just a good choice.

"The audience really do defend Jac to the hilt. I don't do a lot of social media, but I look at my fan mail and I get some lovely, lovely fan mail from people who often say, 'You taught me to be stronger', which is lovely. I am amazed how much people love Jac. Again, the audience are the only people who are party to everything she's been through. I like that they fight for her because she's a fighter and that's what they see, and everybody likes an underdog."

In June 2017, Jac had just begun to thaw towards her half-sister Jasmine Burrows (Lucinda Dryzek), when Jasmine tragically died. "I was really gutted when they told me about that, because there was so much they could have done with [the sisters' relationship], so far they could have gone with it," Rosie says. "I understand why they did it and it makes total sense to me now, but at the time I was thinking, 'She could come back and we could do something else and finally have a relationship'."

Because Lucinda had decided to move on to other opportunities, the producers had to assume that they wouldn't have the option to take the story further. They never recast adult roles, so if Lucinda hadn't been available in the future, they wouldn't be able to bring anyone else in to the role to carry the story on. That being the case, they had to consider the best exit for Jasmine to inform Jac's story going forward.

Rosie says the way it was handled does fit with her character. "Jac doesn't have relationships. She just doesn't. She lost the love of her life—Joseph is and always will be the love of her life, no man has come close. Yes, she had a child with Jonny, but it was probably purely out of convenience and was an accident. Matteo was just a passing fancy— I don't think Jac could ever be with a man who loves himself more than he loves anything else, especially heart surgery, which is her first love.

"The longest-lasting relationship she's had is the one with Sacha, and it's the most important. And I'm desperately trying to convince them to let us move in together, which I think would be wonderful! Because our scheduling conflicts are that Bob [Barrett] and I don't often get to work together, because we're on different wards. So I said, I've got the perfect cure for this—she's a single mum with a kid, he's a single dad with kids. Move them in to a big house together and they can be like *The Odd Couple*, coming in to work in the morning and having little phone calls about what to have for dinner tonight, get caught having that phone call—it'd be wonderful! I've yet to convince them."

Rosie enjoys it when she gets to leave Darwin and work on other wards sometimes. "I've got a week down in AAU next week with Alex [Walkinshaw] and Jaye [Jacobs], who's come back after all this time, and Ellie [Fanyinka] and I'm really desperately looking forward to that, it's going to be lovely. It's just nice to go and play with other people. I've only actually done one scene with Alex since he joined the show and of course we had that whole year together when we were playing lovers on *The Bill*. They did allow us to put a little line in there shortly after he arrived, where I look at him and go, 'Do I know you?', and they let us put that in as a nod to all the *Bill* fans. I'm desperately looking forward to working with him again. He's a lot of fun. But I've been here eleven

154

years and I've pretty much worked with everyone. I started on Keller as a general surgeon, then I did a stint on AAU, then I came up to Darwin. I'm lucky, I've been across everything."

People always want to know whether Rosie ever uses her Jac Naylor persona in real life. She revealed that she did use her Jac "resting bitch face" on some builders who were working on her house. "Jac was channelled last Friday!" she laughed. "It's not often at all I do that. I really am one of these people who leaves my job at work and I go home and spend time with my daughter and my husband and it takes quite a lot for me to have a confrontation with somebody, because I do not like confrontation at all, it makes me feel desperately uncomfortable. Probably mainly because when I do lose my temper it's not pretty. I can't remember the last time I properly lost my temper. It's probably been about fifteen years. My sister [Kelly Marcel] is a writer and we both did very well at school with our English courses and I'm quite erudite, so when I need to put someone in their place I can. So last Friday my builder got it because he decided he wasn't going to turn up to work because he was hungover. Needless to say after I'd finished with him he turned up in half an hour! So I will channel Jac when I need to channel her. I have to admit that my daughter does often get the Jac face. If she's done something terribly bad, she gets the resting bitch face. Yesterday she was yanking on my cat's tail. He's terribly old and he was crying. I was going, 'Beau, don't do that, don't do that,' and she kept doing it, so then she got the, 'Don't. Do. That', and the Face, and she literally started crying. And then I felt very guilty and gave her a cuddle."

Whenever Rosie talks about her daughter Beau her face lights up. She tells me that she struggles with the long hours she has to work. "If you get a director who's lovely and quick and knows exactly what they're doing it's wonderful, because there's an opportunity for you to perhaps finish half an hour early and there's nothing like getting home for bath time, there really isn't, it's the best part of your day. Often I get up in the morning and she's still asleep and I get home at night and she's asleep, so I don't see her at all. There can be a whole week when I haven't actually seen her face, which is horrible. But on the other hand, I worked two days last week and had three days off, and it's the same this week, so it gives and it takes. So I can't really complain. It's a great job."

She says her Holby bosses have always been very helpful if she's needed time off, and particularly feels that Kate Hall is sympathetic to working parents. "She is very concerned with working women, which is great, and I love that."

Rosie has been acting since she was three years old, so she knows the pressures of her job as well as anyone and also has her own way of dealing with it. "It becomes second nature to let it go. If you've had a terribly bad day or if you've fallen out with someone or something like that, it becomes very important to you. Especially here, because this is our other family. I have my home family and I have my work family and my work family are extremely important to me. If you see an injustice here or you upset someone or someone upsets you, it really hurts, and you have to find a way to manage those expectations and remember it is just a job as well. It can be hard to let it go. You really have to have a method. I like to go home and have my cup of tea, then my bath, then I learn my lines, then I come downstairs. I have maybe half an hour to forty-five minutes with my husband, another cup of tea, and I'm up in bed by 9.30–9.45 doing my lines, running them in my head before I sleep. That's my method. If I stick to that, it works, I'm happy. But it can just take one tiny thing and it's ruined your day. I'm quite an emotional person and I take things a little too seriously sometimes."

One time when things did get incredibly hard for her was during the filming of the aftermath of Jasmine's death. "They didn't want me to show my emotions initially," she says. "They specifically wanted me to hold it in and *look* like I was holding it in, and I had to do that for about two and a half weeks before I had a scene where I basically break down with Sacha. They've now cut that scene for other reasons, because of a later storyline. Usually I'm a very controlled person, so having to hold on to my emotions, but also having to have them right there on the edge, just so you can see I'm going to go at any moment, in every scene for two and a half weeks was just exhausting.

"And what happened was, when I got to do this scene where I break, I couldn't stop. I'd worked myself up so much for this amount of time, that when they said, 'Cut', I was still going. I just kept going and kept going and kept going and couldn't stop. And thankfully we only did one take of it and it was fine, and everything just worked out in the one take and I didn't have to do it again. Then I went home after that and I found myself crying again in the evening, because I'd held on to it for such a long time. And that's never really happened to me before. I'm quite good at turning the tears on and off. But I think when you have a child, everything changes in your life and it becomes all-encompassing and your emotions completely change. With that storyline and the holding on to emotions, that was the hardest emotional scene I've ever had to do. Then, when Kate said she was cutting it, I was so upset, until she explained why. Luckily I have the scene, they gave it to me, so I have it if I ever wanted to put it on a showreel or something like that, but it does make me sad that nobody's ever going to get to see it. So yeah, that was definitely the toughest."

The other storyline she found hard to film was saying goodbye to Joseph Byrne. "The last scene with Luke Roberts [13/13 'China In Your Hands' by Martha Hillier]. We're such good friends and we speak all the time and he has promised me faithfully that if I ever leave, he will see me out. He will come back and get me, and I love him for that and it makes me very happy. But that was a tough scene because I was also losing my friend. I joined with Tom [Chambers, who played Sam Strachan] and Luke at the same time and Tom had gone two years before and Luke had stayed and I was gutted at him leaving, absolutely gutted. So that scene in surgery when I was practising my stitching, where he asks me to go with him, that was all real emotions. It was really sad to lose him."

Even though Luke has promised to be part of Jac's leaving story, Holby fans hope that won't happen any time soon. Luckily, Rosie agrees. "I don't see myself leaving, unless something drastic happens," she says. "From what I understand, Jac's one of the most popular characters in Holby, which is wonderful. I just love that everybody loves her. I think people hope she's going to be in each episode, because even though she's this evil character she's also the light relief and people look forward to a bit of light relief in the episodes. We're all replaceable, it's a revolving door and I'm sure I would be forgotten in time and they'd find someone to replace me, but I don't feel like Jac's done yet. I think there's more to do, definitely."

As Rosie says, there's a revolving door of people coming and going at Holby. When I spoke to her she was looking forward to the arrival of Paul McGann as new Darwin consultant John Gaskell, but she was also sad to have recently lost Chizzy Akudolu, who played Mo Effanga. "I'm gutted she's gone, absolutely gutted. We were like Thelma and Louise. I had wonderful scenes with her. In her last episode [19/36 'For the Love of Maureen' by Joe Ainsworth] I had one scene with her, just one, and we both started crying in the middle of the scene and they kept it in, which was very nice. But everything that Jac loves about Mo is said in that one scene, with one line, and you just know that she respects her and she loves her and she's sad that she's going. Chizzy was a wonderful addition. I haven't felt a loss like that in a very long time, since Paul Bradley [Elliot Hope] probably, and before him probably just Luke. Paul and Chizzy both brought a lot of much-needed warmth. She really was the yin to my yang and that's what worked so perfectly. It was a perfect pairing. She would have been one of those people who, if she hadn't had the desire to move on, we'd have been playing off each other for the next ten years. I hope Chizzy will be someone who perhaps drops in every now and again, but I feel like she's going to be one of these people who just doesn't stop working and that's great."

One person who isn't allowed to leave, as far as Rosie's concerned, is Bob Barrett (Sacha Levy). "Bob and I have a little pact. As long as I'm here, he's going to be here. We've agreed to that. If one goes the other one will follow fairly closely. The powers that be don't know that—that'll be interesting for them to read," she laughs. "They're going to have to employ both of us for the rest of their lives."

Rosie has strong views about future romantic relationships for her character. "I think there are women in this hospital and in life who flourish when they're in a relationship, and need a relationship and that comfort and closeness, but I just don't think Jac's one of those people. She just doesn't give herself over emotionally to people. If she needs sex she can go and get that anywhere. I'm wary of making powerful women beholden to the love of a man. I think in this day and age with equality and wage parity it's really important that we don't pigeonhole women, and Jac is the last person in the whole world who needs a man to define her. So when they told me Matteo was coming in I was quite against it at first, until they told me it was going to be very short-lived and I thought that was cool. I was very quick to say to them you don't need to give her a relationship, it's not important, there are other ways to write for her, it doesn't need to revolve around a man. I think it's very important that we point that out to the younger generation that watch this show—that you can be clever and successful and a genius in surgery, and not report to a man. And Jac doesn't really report to anybody. She has her seniors, but she doesn't really report to them. And I want to give that lesson to my daughter—you can do whatever you want to do and it doesn't necessarily have to be based around what a man thinks or wants. So my feeling is she doesn't need it, and that really if it's going to be anyone it's going to be Joseph. And that's it."

JOE McFADDEN (RAF DI LUCCA)

The medicine is the star of the show and that's
the way it should be. – *Joe McFadden*

I talked to Joe in May 2017, after I'd talked to Guy Henry outdoors following the cast photo shoot. It was getting a bit hot in the sun, so we sat in the shade of the peace garden under the Arthur Digby memorial plaque.

I started off by asking him what was happening for Raf in the episodes he was currently filming. "I'm still on Keller and the relationship with Essie is still ongoing," he said. "It's nice to have him settled down with someone for a bit because he's had a string of disastrous relationships, which was fun to play, but it's nice to have him settled."

He said the pace of working on Keller was very different to AAU. "AAU is obviously fast, and pushing gurneys a lot of the time, whereas Keller is much more sedate and it's all electives and doing ward rounds. It's a much slower, gentler pace. It's nice to have had both, because they're very different on screen and with the playing of it. It's nice to get to play with other actors. Much as I enjoy being down on AAU, the thing about being on a specific ward is you only work with those people. For my first three years that I was here I was only with Catherine [Russell] and Alex

[Walkinshaw] and Jemma [Redgrave] and Niamh [Walsh]. It's nice to go and play with Bob [Barrett] and Kaye [Wragg] and David [Ames] and spread my wings a bit. It's nice to move around, but I do love AAU. I think I'm going back there in the next couple of months, because it's really exciting down there."

And Raf was supposed to be a hotshot maxillofacial surgeon and was always making ECMO pumps out of sticky back plastic and stuff, I pointed out. Joe laughed—he has a really infectious laugh. "They never really explored the maxillofacial thing to fruition did they? It was just for that story with Harry [Tressler, played by Jules Knight] in series 17. All of a sudden Raf was this amazing maxillofacial specialist and made Harry look better than he ever looked before, quite frankly," he laughs again, "even after he got pushed off a building!"

In person Joe is absolutely lovely, and I felt guilty that in my blog reviews at the beginning of his time on Holby I always called Raf 'Dr Smug'. I asked him if that had upset him. "I wasn't offended, but it felt like, 'Oh, is that all he is, is he just smug?' There's a fear as an actor that people will take a dislike to you and it felt like you didn't really like the character that much to begin with. I suppose Raf was arrogant, but I quite liked that side to him, when he came in and he was telling everyone off. They wanted him to be quite abrasive and to rub people up the wrong way so that then he would win them round. They do that a lot with new characters—they come in and ruffle all these feathers and within three episodes everyone sees they're really a good guy underneath it all."

I point out that it wasn't long before Holby fans saw another side to Raf, when they started giving him scenes where he was supportive of Serena and the warmth of his character came out (and I had to drop the Dr Smug, because he wasn't). "Which was fantastic, it showed another side to him. Especially with Serena, because she can be very stern and cold but has a real warmth to her. That's why Catherine [Russell]'s such a fantastic actress because she has all of that stuff going on, she's stern and loveable and fallible. I loved all that stuff with her because she's such a great actress, it was a joy to get to work with her. That's the great thing about this show, they have some fantastic people in it and when I get to do scenes with Guy Henry or Hugh Quarshie, you just think these are actors at the top of their game. They have some fantastic actors and it's a real compliment that I'm amongst them. Guy Henry will laugh and giggle until the very last second and then he'll be in it, and he'll be *completely* in it, and it's quite disconcerting to be with. You have to watch him when you're working with him. You can easily just giggle because he's such a funny man."

Joe says it's easy for him to get into the character of Raf. "I watch it sometimes with friends, and they'll say, 'That's Raf. That's Raf's voice now', and I think I have a different voice that I use. He's more bassy than I am. When you've played a character for as long as I have it becomes second nature almost. I read it and I don't have to imagine much how the character's going to react, because I know him almost as well as I know myself, so it's not so much a stretch as it is in the beginning. At the beginning you're thinking, 'Who is this guy? How does he feel about this and about the people around him?' Once you've made those decisions, they're made, unless something big happens. It becomes quite easy in a way."

I asked Joe whether he could see himself staying at Holby long-term, or whether he was getting restless to try new projects. "I'm thinking perhaps I may be coming to the end of my time here. I think it's dangerous for an actor to get comfortable," he said. "It's good to keep challenging yourself. If and when I do go I'll look back on it with real fondness as being a fantastic job that I've really loved. I've worked with some really lovely people." He also said that if and when he did leave, he wouldn't want the door to be left open to him. "I think I would like to die, you know. I don't believe in going back to things. I died in a TV show up in Scotland years ago, a thing called *Take the High Road*. I'd been in it for six years and they said to me, did I want to die? I said, I really do, because it meant the door was slammed closed and could never be opened again. And also it had a bit of impact, it made people sit up and take notice, this character that they'd seen growing up for six years was dead and buried in the woods in a shallow grave, so it had a big impact. And you saw my body! It was quite shocking, actually, for seven o'clock at night, you saw my body being thrown into this grave and the dirt coming in on top of me. So I think I'd like to die."

His favourite part of working for Holby is the medicine. "I've loved the stuff down on AAU. I love it when the medicine is quite intense, when we have those majaxes and there's bodies everywhere. I loved all that. That's when the show is at its best and I think that's why people watch it, because the medicine is fascinating. The things they do in these hospitals on a daily basis is amazing, they're miracle workers. To have someone's life in your hands is such a powerful position to be in and I think that's why the show is as popular as it is. Of course people watch it for the relationships and who we are, but the medicine is the star of the show and that's the way it should be."

More difficult for him is learning the medical jargon. "I got a good tip from Gillian Kearney when I was on *Casualty* a few years ago. She told me to write it on Post-It notes and stick it on the fridge and all around the house, so you're constantly saying it. It's like another language, it's not words that mean anything to you, it's gobbledegook, so you have to learn it by rote. I wake up in the night saying med school terms and get a shower rhyming off all this medical stuff. My neighbours must think I'm nuts. I enjoy all that and when you get your tongue around it, because it's hard, hard stuff to say at the same time as putting a cannula in and opening someone's chest and doing all the physical stuff as well.

"When we're working on the wards there's always a nursing adviser there showing you how to do that stuff properly. If, say, you're doing an eye operation, you'll have an eye specialist there telling you exactly how to hold the scalpel and do the stitches. They pay real attention to that detail. I was talking to a doctor the other day and he said the medical stuff on Holby is spot on. There is some artistic license because we're making a drama, not a documentary, but most of the time they do get it right."

Joe has been acting for most of his life. "I hadn't been to drama school, I just started doing telly from a really young age," he says. "I was twelve when I started on telly up in Scotland, then I was in *Take the High Road* at fifteen. It's brilliant that I'm rubbing up against people like Guy Henry who are fantastic, classically-trained actors, but also completely natural on television as well. The show brings together all these different types of people with their different styles."

LEE MEAD (BEN 'LOFTY' CHILTERN)

When you're delivering the lines it's got to affect you for a reason
and no one can give you that reason apart from yourself.
That's your homework. – Lee Mead

When I talked to Lee he'd just been seen in his first Holby episode. So
what had brought him to Holby after he'd left *Casualty* the year before?
"The main reason was missing the character," he says. "I thought he was
a closed book because I did *Casualty* for two years and they asked me
to stay on longer, which was great, but I've got a daughter, Betsy, who's
seven now. Two years of being in Cardiff during the week and just home
at weekends was really hard. Home is in Southend, so on a Friday night
we'd finish filming at seven, then I'd be driving five or six hours back to
Southend. It was fine for a while but you miss the really important years
and I don't want to miss her growing up. It was a really hard decision
to leave because I was really happy with the job, which was my first
regular TV role. The crew and the cast were amazing and I made friends
for life like Amanda Henderson and Crystal Yu. It was a hard decision
to move on, but I did and went off and made an album, flew a car in
Chitty Chitty Bang Bang for five or six months, did the Palladium panto
at Christmas. I had a great year and a half off and some quality time at
home, then last September Oliver Kent called my agent and asked if I'd

like to have a meeting about playing Lofty again, but for *Holby City*, and I said, 'Wow, absolutely'."

He says he was nervous on his first day at Holby. "I hadn't played the character for almost two years, but after a few scenes I slipped back into playing Lofty and got used to being on set and on camera again. It was nice to have Amanda Henderson as Robyn in my first episode [19/32 'Project Aurous' by Claire Miller]. I thought it was a nice moment of the writer to do that because Lofty needed that little boost. He'd come back as an agency nurse after travelling for a couple of years following what happened in *Casualty* with someone dying. He couldn't face his colleagues and the shame of what happened. He'd only come back to the hospital to get some money to go travelling again. By the end of a very stressful day it's Robyn that makes him feel that actually this is what he loves and what he's meant to be doing with his life."

Lee talked about the following week's episode (19/33 'Enigma' by Peter Mattessi) in which viewers got to find out what had happened to Lofty during his time away. "The two years on *Casualty* it was very much me playing opposite the guest artists that came in and you didn't really get a taste of his past life and who he was, so it's been really nice to shoot this episode," he says, and it's clear how passionate and enthusiastic he is about the storyline. "Ollie [Kent] said how did I feel about playing Lofty gay. I said I had no problems at all, but I didn't want to do the struggles of a gay man coming out, because that's been done a lot of times before. I don't feel you're defined by your sexuality so I wanted it to be very matter-of-fact. They've done a brilliant job on the script for the episode because that's how it unfolds. It's such a great script to be able to do and it really challenged me. I'm not sure if Lofty ever fully questioned his sexuality because he's never had a partner or really been in love. It was a delicate episode to shoot, and the writer did really well."

Lee says his Holby co-stars have made him feel very welcome. "It's been great with Bob [Barrett] and David [Ames] and Kaye [Wragg]. When you're going on to a show with people who've been there already, you rely on the other actors to be open and welcoming and they really were. They were really supportive. Bob was honest and said it could have gone terribly wrong. It's really delicate, relationships that work well on screen and last, but touch wood I think we're creating some good stuff and it's really fun.

"Long hours on set and being in a new environment, it's about having that spark and keeping the energy. We try to have fun on set and keep things light. I think that's how you get the best from the performance. If it's a scene where you have to cry or show some emotion like that you need that time to yourself, but for general stuff it's important to have a good atmosphere on set. The crew are brilliant, they're as much a part of it as we are in terms of having a good and positive energy on set. It makes it so much easier. I've done jobs in the past where it isn't always like that. I'm very lucky."

He feels that coming to Holby has given him new sides of Lofty to explore. "It did concern me that he may end up being just this bumbling guy, because that's part of his character, but now they're writing a whole new side to him. Even the most extrovert people can be very private and very shy and vice versa, sometimes the quietest people are watching everything that's going on. He's looking for love and wants to be happy and wants someone he can be settled with and share his life with, like all of us. That would be something nice to explore. We do get a level of say on the show, we can talk to production about it, and that's not often the case on a lot of shows."

Because Lee had such an extensive background in musical theatre before he started working in TV, I wondered how the two compared. "There's no applause to begin with!" he laughs. "I'm used to getting applause for my work! In theatre you've got that four- or five-week rehearsal period where you can lock down a two-hour show. With *Chitty Chitty Bang Bang* there were dance routines, songs and lots of dialogue and it took hours and hours of study at home and ten hours a day of rehearsal for five weeks to add the layers to the character. It's the same with Lofty as well. Before this episode [19/33] I went away in my own space and gave myself a back story for playing those scenes. You can't just deliver the dialogue, there's got to be a depth to the performance, and layers. When you're delivering the lines it's got to affect you for a reason and no one can give you that reason apart from yourself and that's your homework. In theatre you do that preparation then you open the show to

2,000 people and it's an amazing rush. I still love it, it's a brilliant feeling. The same with a concert performance and delivering a song. With TV it's the same buzz but in a different way, because the camera picks up everything. It's a real challenge because you can't hide, the camera's right there. You're more exposed in TV and the challenge is to ignore the camera and not be conscious of it. Knowing it's picking everything up, but not over-thinking the scene.

"The long days are different as well. My alarm going off at 4.30am!" he laughs. "If you're in a big episode here and your call time is 7.30am, I've got to be up at 4.30am to make sure I'm in on time, and getting back at 8.30 at night. It's sixteen-hour days, so that was a real culture shock. Then lines to refresh. I learned very quickly to do your homework in advance. So you get the script three or four weeks in advance and I try to lock down the episodes really early and learn all the lines, then three weeks later the night before that particular episode, I'll refresh those scenes. The episodes where you're not as featured, it's quieter. You could be in three or four days a week, or half days. It's a great job in that sense because then I'm in the car to do the school pick up for my daughter, which makes me really happy. It's a great work/life balance."

Lee says even though he loves his work, he hopes his daughter won't want to follow in his footsteps. "It's the most insecure profession known to man. But whatever she wants to do, me and her mum will just support it. At the moment she really wants to be a teacher, which is quite sweet. I just want her to be happy really. Whether it's working in a sandwich shop or wanting to be the next prime minister I just want her to have a good work ethic and be happy."

Lee told me about the TV show *Any Dream Will Do*, where he beat 10,000 other auditionees for the role of Joseph in *Joseph and the Amazing Technicolor Dreamcoat*. "That was when I was 25, so before that I'd been acting for about 5 years, but in the chorus of musicals and things like that. *Joseph* was the first musical I ever saw. I was nine and I was mesmerised by the show, as most kids are by that musical. One of my first jobs was in a touring production of it, twelve shows a week around the country. Then I was doing *Phantom of the Opera* in the West End, in the chorus. One Saturday in between shows I was eating my tuna pasta that I made at home and the TV was on. Graham Norton came on, saying, 'Could you be the next Joseph?' And I thought, yes I could. All of us have these defining moments in our lives. I felt so definite and so confident. So that changed my whole career and opened lots of doors."

Even with this high profile he found it hard to get into television, and he credits Oliver Kent with giving him the break. "He's the kindest man and I owe so much of my career in TV to him. I'll be eternally grateful to him. I'd auditioned for *Robin Hood* and *Waterloo Road* and I was getting down to the last stages, but because I had a big theatre background they didn't want to take that risk. Ollie did. I was hugely grateful for that. And then in the first year of *Casualty* to get nominated in the National Television Awards as best newcomer, I was so proud for myself and the character and the show. I didn't win, sadly, but it showed the public had warmed to Lofty, because it's a public vote."

When Lee is sitting in front of you chatting, he doesn't come across as a very extrovert person. It's hard to imagine him getting up on stage in front of a huge audience or performing for the camera. "That's the bizarre thing," he says. "I'm actually quite a shy and very private person, especially in big groups. One to one I'm okay. I don't go to many public events because I find them quite stressful, but I can get up and sing in front of 5,000 people at the Albert Hall. I can lose myself in a song or a character, I can be somebody else. It's a combination of passion and feeling really safe. I feel more safe and confident doing this or on stage, than having to walk into a room with fifty people in it. It's weird isn't it?"

JOHN MICHIE (GUY SELF)

It's fun to play. It's good stuff. It's quite deep. – *John Michie*

John Michie was the first of the Holby actors I interviewed for this book and it was quite a surprise because I didn't even know he was back at Holby until that morning. He was back temporarily to film the storyline leading to Zosia's departure, and he told me about it.

"Guy [Self] is kind of deluded. He's been working in the private sector, but I feel he's back here at Holby because this is the kind of place where he can have some kind of power and do ground-breaking stuff. Also to do with his daughter as well. They have a very strange relationship and he's never wanted her to marry Ollie, who he doesn't think is good enough for her. He's not bright enough, not masculine enough, not anything enough. I'm not sure anyone would be good enough for her. He's caught up in that whole relationship with his daughter marrying someone he doesn't think is suitable. He does quite like Ollie, but he doesn't think he's suitable.

"He's an emotional wreck because he puts his work before everything and always has done, and Zosia holds that against him because he never told her that her mother was dying and the reason that he and the wife agreed not to tell her was because she was at university at the time, so we wanted her to do well and not be distracted. That says it all about Guy—he's absolutely driven by his work. That's why his private life is such an appalling mess and why he's having therapy."

Before John's break from Holby, we discovered more about Guy's background and particularly the awful way he was treated by his monstrous mother (18/45 'Little Acorns' by Johanne McAndrew and Elliot Hope). "That's something he's never got over and in order to suppress that he puts everything into work so he doesn't have to deal with that appalling childhood he had," John says. He didn't know about this back story when he started playing the character. "I knew a little bit about him but not that much. I knew he was going to have to deal with his daughter's bipolar situation and part of the reason he came to the hospital was that he needed to be around her and help her and support her. But I feel as if you're never quite sure who's the parental figure and who's the child. Sometimes underneath the bluster and bravado and macho front he presents there's a frightened little boy really, which goes back to the mother and the abuse he suffered. So in this story you'll see Zosia is concerned about him and trying to help him, while he's trying to destroy her relationship with Ollie. It's weird."

John says he loves playing the villain. "They're always much more interesting to play. All villains are essentially weak people who are trying to cover over something in their past or something inadequate that they feel about themselves. The thing to find in every character is their flaw and that's what's interesting. If someone is nice all the time that's not very interesting to do," he laughs. "A villain has multiple flaws and that's what's interesting for an actor to get a hold of. Why is this person like that? Why are they behaving like that? He sees himself as doing the right thing to help his daughter and promote her career. He doesn't see the Machiavellian side. That's also a part of his mental illness, that he can't quite see reality, but it's hardly surprising with the upbringing he's had. He's covering all the time—the bravado, the flirting, the drinking, 'I'm the best neurosurgeon, I'm a world leader,' all that stuff. It's just hiding something within him that he's never properly addressed. He's tried to address it in therapy and realises that he needs to, but he also wonders whether his daughter's mental illness is hereditary. He'll wonder about those things, but he's never had a long discussion with Zosia about mental illness, because he feels there's a stigma about it even within the medical profession."

It always felt like Guy was in a sense ashamed of Zosia's illness and saw it as weakness, and John agrees. "That's why early on in our story he took her to a hospital to recuperate and have psychotherapy, a private place where he could shut it away. So yes, he does feel shame. He feels that Guy and Zosia should be the leading lights in their field all the time and everyone should look up to them. He has unrealistic expectations not only of himself but of his daughter, which is why she finds him so difficult to be with. It's fun to play, though. It's good stuff. It's quite deep."

John explained how he got into the character of Guy Self. "Any character I play I use myself, because you're trying to present a truthful character and the only truth you know is your life experience. So I find something in my life that fits into something in his life and once you have that connection it's a really easy emotional hook. The time when I had the breakdown, when Guy started to talk about his mother and he started to open out and he burst out crying and all this stuff came out—to make a man like that be as weak and vulnerable as I had to make him, you find something in your life. At the time my mother happened to be ill, though she's all right now. As an actor you have to recognise that you prostitute yourself in a way. You have to get out your emotions through another character. It's actually quite cathartic, it makes you feel good because you get stuff out. So that's how it works: you think, 'What do I have in my life that's similar?', and you recall that emotion and use that. You can do it quite quickly. I don't need to sit in a corner.

"When I had to do the breakdown [18/45 'Little Acorns' by Johanne McAndrew and Elliot Hope] I kind of did keep myself to myself and you can make yourself feel a bit lonely. It's all versions of Stanislavsky, Method acting. There are extreme versions you can go to if you're Robert De Niro, or there are levels I'll go to without sending myself completely nuts, so you use little tricks like that. So you don't go and chat to other people and have coffee, you keep yourself to yourself and then you walk on the set and you're ready to go. You try and hold that emotion in until the take and then let it out, but preferably not in the wide shot, which is why

I asked them to shoot the close first, because if you let everything go in the big wide they're not going to use it. They use it maybe at the beginning of the scene and the end of the scene. So what happened was we shot the wide and I was trying to hold it back and I could feel it just coming out, so I said to the director [Steve Brett], 'Can you go in for the extreme close-up?', which I knew they would use in a scene like that, and I let it all go and it all happened. Then he went wider and it all happened again—I was feeling quite emotional that day! Then you turn around and you've got to do it for the other actors, so I had to give that to Camilla, when the camera wasn't on me, as much as you possibly can, which is never going to be exactly how you did it in the take. It's quite exhausting. At the end of it you're like, ugh, God, empty.

"I enjoyed that day. Finally the father breaking down, for the daughter to see he's actually as vulnerable, if not more vulnerable, than her. Zosia is seeing her dad just blubbing his heart out, which I don't think she'd have done before. So because that situation was new to the characters, it was very exciting to get that emotion out in a believable way, which is not easy. You do have to work at it, you've got to be in the right place and do all the right things that day to make sure you can break down. And when it works it's great.

"I said to the director beforehand, 'I'm not going to cry in this scene, I'm just warning you now'. That's the best thing to say. If you try to make yourself cry it won't work, but if you try and stop yourself from doing it and you use the emotion and hold it, then it will happen and it did. There's lots of little tricks that you work out after years in this business. Music can help. You just find a track that gets you going. And then for the take you're emotionally on the starting block. None of it's difficult."

John is a very experienced actor who has worked on a number of soaps including a long stint on *Coronation Street*. I asked him how Holby compares. "I've done a few soaps and you churn it out and it's on multi-camera so you can't really light it and you can't assist the drama with the lighting and the shots, it's basically very simple shots, very simple lighting. So because of that it's a very fast turnover and you're moving very quickly, but you can't give it the drama look that Holby has. It's a huge ask to produce fifty-two hours of drama a year. I don't think there's any other TV company in the world that does it. And they're BBC hours, the full sixty minutes. An ITV 'hour' of drama is forty-seven or fifty minutes [because of ad breaks] and that's a big difference, shooting another fifteen minutes of drama every week. It's hard to keep standards up, but on the whole they do on Holby. Everything is down to the scripts and the writing. The scripts are where the real work is done. You can make something better, but you can't make it good if it's not good in the first place. So Simon [Harper] and Kate [Hall] do a really good job making sure that happens."

HUGH QUARSHIE (RIC GRIFFIN)

[*Holby City*] is, by definition, part of the national cultural diet and
I'm very pleased and very proud to be part of it. – *Hugh Quarshie*

Hugh Quarshie has played Ric Griffin since 2001, making him by far
Holby City's longest-serving cast member.

"There are many good reasons for staying here," he says. "Of course
I've thought every year about moving on and there are powerful reasons
for perhaps leaving and thinking about doing other things. I left two
years ago to return to the Royal Shakespeare Company to do *Othello* and
I'm very glad I did it, but it was very arduous, although it was critically
successful.

"My reasons for staying at Holby are not just because of the regularity
of income, though that is a significant factor! There are a number of
reasons. One, millions of viewers watch it so it is, by definition, part
of the national cultural diet and I'm very pleased and very proud to be part
of it. Two, Holby and *Casualty* have always consistently had a fairly high
proportion of the cast who are so-called BAME—Black Asian Minority
Ethnic—and three, I think we do have a bearing on the standard of
pre-watershed screen writing. A lot of people say continuing drama is just
a euphemism for 'soap', and I can understand why, there are soap operatic

elements in Holby, but at the same time I like to think that we aspire always to raise the bar. Historically we have tackled some heavy subjects, interesting subjects, and I hope that we continue to do so."

He says another factor is that he's developed a relationship with the producers whereby they trust his instincts about the scripts. "I believe they're quite thrilled when I do change something or say something in a way that hadn't been expected. It keeps it interesting for me and real for them. From my point of view it is set in a hospital which has surgical wards and I look forward to those scenarios where surgery is the spine of the story and the relationships are the ribs, if you like, off the spine. I think it's my responsibility to be, not idiosyncratic for the sake of it, but to be behaviourally and psychologically true to the character and to myself. So that for me is what keeps it interesting. I've often said it's a much greater test of an actor's skill to deliver a line of mind-numbing banality like, 'Ricky I really, really love you', for example, as opposed to 'Perdition catch my soul but I do love thee!', which is what Othello says about Desdemona. The poetry pretty much does a lot of the work for the actor. But if you can move the audience with something as banal as 'Ricky I really, really love you', then you're doing your job well. So I relish those opportunities. If I can't do it, then I might finesse the line. And finessing, in my vocabulary, means anything from changing a word to rewriting the line, or sometimes rewriting the scene, but I shouldn't say that too loudly.

"My guide is that every line has to be said in a characteristic way. Even the medical information, you've got to find a way of delivering that line in the way your character would deliver it—the tone, the inflection. Sometimes maybe just changing the grammar slightly. When you hear the line you've got to think only that character could have said that line. To a large extent you have to interpret what the writer wants and interpret the stage directions. So there is a certain amount of personalisation of the lines. Occasionally, where the script has been through several drafts, you might notice a jump in tone or something that doesn't quite fit, so that can be altered in rehearsal.

"And when I say 'rehearsal', our rehearsals last minutes because we can't hang around. Today we've got four or five scenes to shoot. You can't hang around discussing it too much. But if you get the feeling the director is asking you to do something which is principally for the camera and is not character motivated, I think it's not just your right but your responsibility to say, 'Wait a minute, this doesn't feel quite right'. By and large they've cast actors with good instincts, actors of repute and occasionally of renown, so it would make sense if they listened, because this isn't born out of ego, it comes from a sense of care and responsibility and indeed out of a sense of dedication and love. We do care about what we do."

Hugh has directed an episode of Holby in the past (16/33 'Crush' by Glen Laker), and he found it a difficult experience. "In my pretentious naiveté I'd identified some themes in this script and wanted to reflect those themes in image systems. There was a theme of matriarchy and a theme of the jungle and I wanted whenever possible to shoot outside, through foliage. But then the producer said it would save time if we shot the scene indoors." He laughs. "That's the reality of it—you think that's one image system gone, so maybe I can move a pot plant! You realise fairly quickly it is about compromise and thinking on your feet. I realised the director's job is just to take a decision and I was beating myself up thinking was it the right decision. In a way, that's not the point. There's a number of ways of shooting a scene and I learned that. There are also things that can be fixed in the edit if you've missed a shot, you can take bits from different takes and work around it. A good team will help a director get through it and eventually a director will acquire enough instinct and experience to know what shots they need. I think next time round I'd be more relaxed about it."

Hugh remains interested in the directorial process and appreciates watching other directors work. "There are some directors who've been here as long as I have and I've watched them grow. Jamie Annett, for one. And you just notice the things they do, like lowering the camera angle, starting on feet and coming up on a face. Now of course we can use drones. Drone photography can help you tell a story. If you use it well and creatively you can get both character and a sense of context. You can focus on someone's face, pull out, and see where you are. There was recently a good shot of Hanssen standing on the roof of the hospital, for example, and that was a drone shot. There was a time when the way a scene was shot was pretty much determined by the size of your TV set. With a small screen it was invariably master shot, close up, close up. But now people have got huge great television screens and HD and you can shoot it like a film and come in for detail and pay much more attention to the lighting. You can create an atmosphere which adds to the story. You can show someone close up who might be having personal problems and then pull out and show a very busy ward going on around them, to emphasise that even in the middle of it all they're starkly alone."

Sometimes he gets frustrated with the way things change in post-production. "There was an episode which started with Griffin sitting on a bench barefoot, tapping his foot in time to some music he was listening to. I had suggested a particular piece of music to the director and producer, a piece of Ghanaian music which seemed appropriate. Nobody but a Ghanaian would know the lyrics meant, 'He's walking on the ground and he's barefoot'. It's a way of saying he hasn't got much to show for himself, so it was kind of apt. It had a specific beat and I was tapping my foot to that beat. And in post, they decided to put in some Suzanne Vega-type music, so I suddenly looked like the only black man in Holby who had no sense of rhythm!" He laughs. "I was not happy about that! That sort of thing can be frustrating. But I like to think it's never about ego. It's about making the scene work."

JEMMA REDGRAVE (BERNIE WOLFE)

I'm very attached to everyone here. It's a lovely
place to work. – *Jemma Redgrave*

I could hear the cheers and applause from the fifth floor. The cast and crew had been outside in the car park all morning, filming a fun-run sequence for 19/44 ('Go Ugly Early' by Nick Fisher). The sound of the starter klaxon could be heard repeatedly as the race was filmed again and again. There were dogs involved in the race too, so there was an occasional bark. Joe McFadden (Raf Di Lucca) and Ayesha Dharker (Nina Karnik) both said the dogs they were working with were lovely and they wished they could keep them.

The cheers and applause at the end of filming were for Jemma Redgrave, because the fun run was the last scene she filmed as Bernie Wolfe for now. Half an hour later she appeared in the fifth-floor office, tired and worn out but very kindly taking some time to sit down with me and talk about her time in Holby, and especially how she was feeling after her last scene.

"It is emotional. I'm very attached to everyone here. It's a lovely place to work," she said. "There's a cornucopia of reasons that meant this is the right time to go, but it's very hard. That last scene was lovely because so many of the actors I've been working with were involved, so I got to play my last scene with a lot of the actors from Keller as well as AAU and the lovely SAs I've been working with who are fantastic, and great crew. So it's been great."

I asked how Bernie's story would end. "It doesn't end," she says. "But she feels that her heart is with Serena and it's also with the military and I think she's a bit of a gypsy and finds it hard being in one place for too long. So it's up sticks, take up the tent pegs, pack up the tent and move on. She doesn't go back to the army, but she's going back to a military field hospital. Via Serena."

She says the success of the storyline about Serena and Bernie surprised her, "but of course it makes complete sense, because I realise now that there are a lot of male gay relationships in the culture around us, but there aren't so many female gay relationships, and particularly not female gay relationships of women our age. A lot of the response I got to the storyline was that if and when there were lesbian relationships on telly or film they were often tragic. A lot of people felt they were under-represented and I think it meant a lot to a lot of people that they felt themselves represented on screen. We had a lot of messages from young women who said it had given them the courage to come out. They told their parents that seeing this relationship develop on screen had given them a great deal of courage to live the lives that they wanted to live. I've had messages from people, and I think it's very brave of these young women to even write. Maybe partly getting something down on paper to somebody you don't know, but you feel you have a connection to, is part of taking stock and thinking in a different way about how to handle difficult feelings."

She says that Holby has been "the most tremendously positive experience. What they do here is bring people in for six months and they see how the character sits in the hospital. When you put two people together they may not have chemistry on screen, but there was chemistry and it worked well between Catherine [Russell] and I. We worked well together as actors as well. We're very different in our approach to our work, but in a way that complemented each other well. Catherine has a great deal of impressive notes in her script and I wish I did, but I don't. I tend to think mine through. But in our different ways we come to the moment and we both seem to be in the moment at the same time and that works very well."

Jemma didn't rule out a future appearance of Bernie back at Holby. "It's in the lap of the gods and the producers. They're not killing me off! I'm grateful to have worked with a really first-class crew and an across-the-board cast of really marvellous actors and producers and writers and directors who all care so passionately. Fifty-two weeks of the year, it's no mean feat to create work of such quality. That is so, so impressive and it's been so marvellous to be a part of it."

One question that Holby fans had asked me to ask her was whether she'd ever consider appearing on *Strictly Come Dancing*. She responded by singing, "I can't dance, don't ask me, I can't dance, don't ask me," and laughing. "I think the humiliation that my family, friends and I would go through is of such extremity that I would be persuaded by everybody not to. I think I'd be out before I got to week one."

I didn't want to keep her any longer, because she was obviously exhausted from filming and the emotions of the day and I was sure she'd have people she'd want to speak to before she left.

"I feel like I'm talking absolute nonsense," she said. "I feel as old as Methuselah. I feel like I've had my spine removed. I think that's the toughest thing about this job, that sometimes you don't have time to come up for air. Usually when you do these kind of hours for a period of time, this is the actor's thing, somehow your immune system holds together until the end of the job and then, it's cliché and classic, but you get sick. Literally there was a finish line down there [for the fun run] and I ran through it, and I think it's had a physical impact. I feel completely shattered, so I apologise if I'm talking nonsense. I don't even know how I'm going to get home in one piece. I think I'd better take it really slowly and do back roads. I'll get into the car and go home and collapse on the sofa in a damp heap. It's very sad."

CATHERINE RUSSELL (SERENA CAMPBELL)

I think the gap between myself and Serena has probably
got smaller over the years. – *Catherine Russell*

I talked to Catherine on the phone while she was happily 'thumb twiddling' during her break from Holby, managing to catch her before she set off to travel around Europe by camper van.

The first thing we talked about was how Serena had changed during her time on the show. "I think she's softened somewhat," Catherine said. "When I was brought in it wasn't exactly as a Connie [Beauchamp] replacement, because that would be impossible, but to have that sort of weight behind her. I was brought in very much as a foil for Ric, and she was a hard-headed businesswoman as well as a brilliant surgeon. And although it wasn't explicitly written, I always imagined she was rather right wing. A sort of Joan Rivers with a bit of Margaret Thatcher thrown in. The sort of person you'd love to sit next to at dinner, but who probably wouldn't be your best mate. And she was very pragmatic and concerned with number crunching and making sure beds weren't blocked. Obviously very intelligent, but very pragmatic. More head than heart. Over the years that has changed somewhat, although I do like to remind the writers now and again, please don't make her a liberal softie, because she's not, and never will be. What's interesting about playing a long-running character, which is something I've never done before, is that inevitably you end up bringing more of yourself to the part than might otherwise be the case and I think the gap between myself and Serena has probably got smaller over the years. When people say, are we like our characters? – yes, in a way we're all sort of exaggerated versions of our own selves. To play a character so very far away from yourself for such a long period of time would be extremely difficult."

Serena has had some very gruelling storylines, including her mother Adrienne's dementia and death, and then the death of her daughter Elinor. Catherine says the Adrienne storyline was the hardest for her to play. "I'm sure if I had had a child of mine die, then that would have been the hardest storyline, but thank God I haven't. But I have had a mother die. So the Elinor storyline was very much my imagination of how that would be, and that was actually very difficult to play because I've got no idea how anybody even begins to stay standing after the death of a child. I had to just try and imagine what that was like. The death of a mother and a mother getting ill… My mother didn't have dementia so I was saved that, but she did die when she was only seventy so it was a rather young death. I found myself being more affected personally by that storyline than I did by the Elinor storyline. Also Sandra Voe [who played Adrienne] and I got on like an absolute house on fire and I really, really loved working with her. Rather like Jules Robertson [Jason Haynes], she was only initially booked in for one episode, but because she was so brilliant and so well loved, they just continued writing for her. She's just one of those extraordinary people who spreads love wherever she goes. I think Holby's brilliant in that way. If somebody comes in and they do a really fabulous job and they also fit in with the family that Holby is, if they can they will continue to write for them. So that was the hardest, but possibly also the most rewarding, storyline to do."

The storyline affected a lot of people, and Catherine still gets people coming up to her and talking about it. "There was a woman outside the supermarket a couple of days ago collecting for people who are unpaid carers, and she'd started this charity and I just chucked some coins in the tin as you do and she rushed up and said, 'I have to say that storyline with your mother and being a carer helped me through, when I was at home looking after my mother before she died. Seeing your character allowed to be angry and frustrated made me feel better about my frustrations and made me feel not quite such a bad person'. That was great, because that storyline was years ago now and it still touches people. When that happens it's very heartening."

Of course the storyline that has touched people massively recently has been the Bernie/Serena love story. "That storyline has really taken off," Catherine says. "It has a life of its own outside the show, literally. There are many, many, many fans of that storyline who are now friends with each other, meet up with each other, help each other out and are each other's safety net for what the world may be throwing at them. Lesbian representation is so rare, particularly on a mainstream, pre-watershed television show, that people were thrilled to see it, and rightly so. It's extraordinary in this day and age that I have to be saying they were thrilled to see it, but they were, and it's had the most remarkable, positive effect on many people's lives, I think. I've met a lot of these women now, Berena fans. I did a play, *What the Butler Saw*, earlier this year and hundreds came from all over the world and they feel incredibly invested in the Berena storyline."

I asked Catherine if she'd missed Holby while she was away. "No. I haven't. I've missed some of the people, but I've seen Ellie [Fanyinka], Jemma [Redgrave], Joe [McFadden], Lucy [Dryzek]. We keep in touch because we all get on so well. But five years of that schedule... People should never moan about being employed to pretend to be somebody else, you know—it's nice work if you can get it. Although when you've got a busy storyline the hours are horrendous, up at five o'clock in the morning and you're home half past eight at night. However, that's not every day. If you split your hours over an entire year it's about three days a week and you're paid when you're not going in, so any actor who starts moaning about their timesheet needs a smack. However, it's not the timing so much. It's that five years of always carrying at least three, sometimes four, occasionally five stories in your head is tiring. Even when you're not at work you're learning lines. There's no headspace. Even though you might not be at work, you might be tending your garden but you're still thinking and you're still having to pick up scripts and you're still having to learn. So after five years of no headspace, I sort of felt a bit worn out if I'm honest, and my batteries really needed to recharge. I jumped straight into another project. I finished that play in April, so for the first time in five and a half years there are nobody's words in my head but my own. And that's quite thrilling! That's not to say I'm not looking forward to getting back. I will be desperate to get back by October, I'll be bored with myself. I'm sure I'll be absolutely gasping to get back to work and to be busy and to have my head full of somebody else's words."

Several people had mentioned to me how well Catherine prepares her scripts, so I was interested to find out more about her working method. "I don't think acting's easy for me," she says. "If I don't work hard, I'm not particularly good. I like to be on top of the script, I like to know what's coming up and where I've been. For me anyway it's pretty difficult to play a scene accurately if you don't know where you've been or where you're going. We film completely out of order and out of sequence. I like to make decisions that aren't necessarily instinctive, because I think sometimes the first option that my brain comes up with isn't necessarily the most interesting. I give it some thought and try and work out how that particular scene can relate to something that's happened in my past, or where it's coming up or that sort of thing. From an emotional point of view I like to try and work at it. Everyone's different. Some people do no preparation at all and are completely brilliant. If I did no preparation at all I would be rubbish. So that's why I do it. I also can't bear not knowing my lines properly. I don't want to be sitting in a scene going, 'What do I say next?' I want to be thinking the thoughts that Serena is thinking, not thinking the thoughts Catherine is thinking. So that's another reason why I write notes. I also find it helps me learn it, so my scripts are covered in drawings and notations and things like that. I change lines quite a bit, but I always run it past the producers first. I can't bear it when lines rhyme, for instance. I hate an unintended rhyme. When you have to produce fifty-two scripts a year, often writers don't have the time or the luxury to hear their words spoken out loud, and often what looks fantastic on a page doesn't sound like real dialogue. And you know in life if somebody says something that rhymes, immediately everyone goes,

'Oh! I'm a poet and didn't know it!' It's really rare in ordinary speech for something to rhyme, so I'm a stickler for that sort of thing. I've always done it. There have been a few times in my career when I haven't and I've regretted it. So it's not to say it's right or that's how anybody else would do it, but it's just the way I do it."

Catherine summed up how she feels about working on Holby. "I've never worked on another continuing drama, but I think what's unique about the Holby experience is this notion of family. It's this idea that when they cast an actor they're not just casting the person who's best for that role, they're casting the person who's best for that role who will fit in, and appreciate being there, who won't moan, who's going to turn up and do the job properly and be part of that community. And the community extends from saying good morning to the guys on the gate, to the runner offering to bring you a cup of tea, to the director and the people who are working in the office. If you're going to be one of those actors who's going to mess about and not be considerate to everybody and appreciate that this is absolutely a team effort, you won't last long. And I love it for that. People care about each other. And the thing about the longevity of a job like that is that because you know you're all going to be together for such a long time you know you have to get on with each other. There's no point in finding people's eccentricities irritating because, rather like a family member, you've got to find a way and a strategy of making sure that everyone gets on with each other. You know that you're going to be with some of these people for at least a year, so people make the effort. It's a very pleasant working atmosphere. Frictions arise, of course they do, but nine times out of ten they're solved pretty quickly."

CHRISTIAN VIT (MATTEO ROSSINI)

When I get inside the studios now I'm already the character,
even if I'm walking on the alleyways. – Christian Vit

Christian Vit greets me by kissing me on both cheeks, "because I'm Italian", and like the character he plays he seems to rather enjoy playing up to the Italian stereotype.

"Matteo is an Italian cardiothoracic surgeon, very well travelled and very well spoken," he says. "He's from the Marche region of Italy and he's named after the composer Gioachino Rossini, that's why he's supposed to have this artistic way of approaching the surgery. When an artist masters the rules he's able to break them and to find different paths. That's Matteo. He's brave, he's assertive, he has a very soft human side, but it's always covered by this macho, assertive, cocky aspect. There's a lot of soft sides to him if you dig deep."

I met him while episodes were being screened that introduced Matteo's wife (played by Ayesha Dharker) and the back story about the loss of their son. "Previously he's been all very smiley and charming and joking, being always on the edge of being kicked out of the hospital by Jac Naylor and playing this cat and mouse game with her. But that was just one part of him. Now we see his past coming back. It's tough for him to face things again and probably face them properly for the very first time. Usually when things get hot for Matteo in an emotional way he tries to sneak away. He has a strong moral sense and his main focus is to save lives. In every circumstance he has to accomplish his duty as a doctor. In Italian this is called *giuramento di Ippocrate*," or the Hippocratic oath, though it does sound a lot nicer in Italian.

Christian then reveals that I may not have been talking to Christian at all. "When I get inside the studios now I'm already the character, even if I'm walking on the alleyways," he says. "I've never left my character 100%. The 85% of Matteo is always sticking on me. Just when I leave the studios I'm Christian. It just happens naturally, you don't have to push for that. You get used to being in this building to play the character, so as soon as you step in the building the character gets inside you. I'm not going to fight that, it's a nice thing." It's the first time Christian has worked on a long-running series, so the experience is new to him. "What you have to do at the beginning is basically listen to yourself according to what you're given as a storyline. We're a team here and I'm always very happy to hear what the directors, who are more experienced than me, can give me as a suggestion, and I take the best out of everything. Every actor has to craft his own method and the only thing that matters really is that it works on the screen. You have to find your own recipe. I'm still finding mine. It's always a work in progress, which makes this work very fascinating, because you never end up being complete. You always have something to improve, you always have something to find out. It's like playing an instrument." He pauses and then adds, laughing, "That's a very Matteo thing to say!"

He's obviously having a lot of fun playing the role. "From an acting point of view he's a very enjoyable character," he agrees. "We Italians have our own humour which is maybe different than the English one, so I'm never sure whether an English audience will get my humour or not. I'm always trying to find the right way to deliver the humour and the fun, but it seems like it's been quite well received from that point of view. I had some scenes with Chizzy [Akudolu] that were very funny. I love comedy so when there's a chance for me to make people laugh, I'm always happy. But I'm also happy to go into the darker side. As an actor you're told that to know how to cry 100% you need to know how to laugh 100%. I try to cover all of the range as much as I can. You try to give the truth to the audience. So when I was crying listening to the music box [19/28 'Past Imperfect' by Becky Prestwich] I was delivering a truth of myself as an actor. I'm not going to say what I was thinking of, but it was something as specific as the character was living at that moment. I just hope the audience got that it was a genuine emotional thing. That, for me as an actor, is enough."

He says that by training and practice he can get into an emotional scene, but not take it home with him afterwards. "It takes a while to trigger the emotions and a while to release them afterwards. I allow myself ten minutes to get rid of that, but here we have to move on to the next scene, so you have to be quick, true and flexible. You have a crew waiting for you, and it's crucial to have the respect of all the team, so the sooner the better. As you go on it affects you less. You get used to it."

Having Italian as his first language has helped Christian with the medical jargon on the show. "The medical thing is not easy but it makes my life easier than the others because of being Italian, it's quite easy for me to say the medical terms. The Latin root helps me. When it comes to being in the operating theatre and delivering the truth there, it's like the musical box, you have to be aware what you're doing. That's why all the medical advisers and all the team are doing a great job. At a certain time the words become secondary. When you're believing what a person is doing sometimes you don't pay attention to what the words are, it's how it's delivered. So I'm more focused on what I'm doing and I want to be compelling as a surgeon. Which is not easy, because I've never operated on anybody in my life!"

He has an interesting observation about the operating theatre scenes, which none of the other actors mentioned. "The drawback is that after half a day or a day spent in the operating theatre you feel really, really tired," he says. "It's like you're not breathing the same way. You have the mask, the hat, the gloves, the gowns, the scrubs, and it's more physically demanding. After a day in the operating theatre I feel twice as tired as when I'm shooting in the ward. I totally enjoy it though."

He watched real surgeons at work as part of his preparation for the role, and what impressed him the most was how calm everything was. "The atmosphere you feel is like being in an office. Everything is very smooth and even relaxed, even though there's a patient with an open chest there, because what they're doing is something they're very used to, they're very confident about and there's nothing to worry about. So it's not something major to them, like a normal human would expect. When I was there I was astonished—in a good way—at how natural things are. For me it was a major thing because it was the first time I witnessed it, but for the surgeons it's not, and I'm glad it's not because it seems like they know what they're doing. So in theatre scenes at Holby we try to put across this feeling that it's business as usual. There are moments where the situation gets a little bit difficult, of course. I had that scene with Matteo and Serena Campbell [19/25 'Unbreakable' by Elliot Hope and Johanne McAndrew] where the patient died. In another episode I had to take Chizzy away from her patient who died [19/30 'Gold Star' by Ed Sellek]. So there are moments that are quite emotionally strong. Surgeons are not gods. My character is someone who likes to know what's going on all the time, but there's always the 0.0001% that can go wrong. You never know. You take the risk and you have to let it go if it doesn't work out. That's another part of being a surgeon—being detached from what happens to the patient. If someone dies in your hands and you've done the best you could, it was just meant to be. You can't let it affect you, otherwise you won't operate again."

Christian admits that it wasn't easy to watch a real operation. "I was afraid I would pass out. I started to get closer and closer just to feel the reaction. The surgeon told me that every student they get into the operating theatre, they don't know the reaction. The very first cut is with a scalpel. As soon as the scalpel hits the skin, a lot of people just pass out. Then you have the diathermy which cuts deeper and it burns, which makes a smell that's very uncomfortable. I think I'm more sensitive to the smell. When I smelled that burnt skin, burnt meat smell, I was feeling a little sick. I didn't pass out. At a certain point instead of looking directly in the patient's chest I was sitting on a little stool at the side and there was a camera focusing on the surgery so it was clearer what I was seeing, but at the same time it was creating a little bit of detachment, even though the patient was physically there." Was he channelling Matteo so he didn't pass out? He laughs. "Oh no. Matteo would have just been saying to the other surgeons, 'I'm here now. You can go'."

As I discovered while I was at Holby, the storyline can change at fairly short notice. Christian enjoys that aspect. "It's always a work in progress. There's a discovery to be made every day when I read the script, because sometimes you're told some stuff and then it turns out to be something else. It's quite nice to discover it little by little, it's challenging and you have to be flexible. It's quite intriguing when you're always discovering something new."

Christian loves living in London. "I was born in Venice. It's a very interesting city to have been brought up in. That's why I'm a bit of a Marco Polo myself, always exploring. I've been living in London for three years and I'm super happy. I was living in Rome before because if you want to pursue a career as an actor in Italy there's no way you can stay in Venice. The work happens in Rome, a little bit in Milan, but Rome is the base for actors in Italy. Then I decided to make the move to London, and I wished I'd come before. I love London, it's an amazing place, the opportunities are incredible. I've worked on movies in Italy and a couple of projects here, but mainly TV. Now is a golden age for TV. Holby itself is very well looked after from a technical point of view, the way it's shot, there's a lot of care and hard work. And you can tell that when you watch the programme. That's why Holby is such a well-respected series."

ALEX WALKINSHAW
(ADRIAN 'FLETCH' FLETCHER)

I'd stay till all my hair falls out. I'd have a tiny bit of quiff left, just at the front. More like Homer Simpson, I'm thinking. – *Alex Walkinshaw*

"I love Fletch," senior nursing adviser Lisa Spencer-Blackshaw told me. "Because he's such a good nurse and he's so like real-life male nurses. Everybody loves the male nurses in hospital."

Alex Walkinshaw has played Fletch since 2012, first in *Casualty* and now in *Holby City*. He describes Fletch as "a bit like glue between people. One of his skills is to big-brother people, put an arm round them. It's just as important as diagnosing and treating something medical. He talks to everyone in the same way. He's a good leveller. He has emotional authority because he's been through his own issues."

When we met he was looking forward to his character getting a promotion to director of nursing, and locking horns with Jac Naylor. "I think Fletch is a very different kettle of fish to her," he says. "She's very used to having a man standing opposite her desk, to attention, while she's sitting telling them off and letting them know exactly how the land lies. As a woman she intimidates the hell out of him, as a surgeon he knows she's great, she's the head of the department etcetera, but he finds the confidence in himself to say, 'Who are you talking to like that? Don't talk to my nurses like that. Don't talk to *me* like that. You're not my boss'. And she's not. So I think it's going to be interesting to play that, because everyone's very intimidated by Jac Naylor and I don't know if Fletch is going to be. Hopefully there's going to be a lot of head clashing and some nice scenes. I think he'll bring a bit of normal-speak to the boardroom, something we can understand. He's a bit of a problem solver and an Everyman."

We've often seen Fletch's children sharing scenes with him, and they're always brilliant to watch, particularly Macey Chipping as Evie and Kai O'Loughlin as Mikey. Alex sounds genuinely enthusiastic when he says, "I love those Fletchlings. They're just stunning, they're absolutely brilliant, all of them. Macey is extraordinary. She's such a lovely actor and a really nice girl. Straight away we sort of bonded. I'm a bit of a wally, as a rule. Having two kids of my own I'm a serious dad and strict, but I'm goofy and I'm up for fun and games and sarcasm, so I try to make a real effort with all of them to get that connection with them. It just gets repaid every time we do scenes together. If I could work with them all the time it would be lovely. Kai lives fifteen minutes from where I grew up, so he's like a little Fletch on a hot wash. All we've got to do is grow that hair and tease that quiff and he's me. His mum and dad are very similar to people I know from where I grew up, and he's really great. They all listen and we have conversations and they ask me if they can try this and I say yeah, just go for it. And they come up with great ideas and it just works. They're all just adorable, they're really nice kids, and it's a joy to have them around."

Alex says there are a lot of similarities between Fletch and himself, though he thinks he's a more serious person than the character he plays. "Fletch is so high-energy, always moving. I'm not quite like that," he says. "People don't always see me being quiet on set because I find it easier to stay up all day than to go up and down, up and down. It's not method acting at all, but I kind of adopt more of his personality from the line run. When I get on set, I start to be more like that. It's exhausting, but it's less exhausting than picking myself up, putting myself down. I blur it from the moment I get on to set. And then I can get into the thinking of it a little bit easier. There are lots of similarities between me and Fletch, because I can be like that, as energetic and high-energy, but when I'm at home I'm someone's dad and someone's husband and my life has to carry on, there's things I have to do and think about, so I'm a lot more serious at home."

I wondered how it had been playing a high-energy person who was confined to bed and almost paralysed, in the storyline at the end of series 18 where Fletch was stabbed. "That was more emotional because he had more emotional things going on. Physically he was stuck in bed, he couldn't walk. It kind of helped and I found myself falling asleep in scenes when I didn't have things to do because I would just have to be still! But they were emotional storylines. The stillness and the frustration of being still, for Fletch. All of his focus was on, what if he never walks again? He's on his own, he's got four children, and it was always about the children, to the point where he asked Raf to take them on if anything happened to him. So it was helpful to be still on those scenes and let the emotions wash over me and come out of me. Your body's still, but your brain's 100 miles an hour.

"It was a really nice storyline and because they've got such nice actors here and we're all such good friends we all really, really get on. That helps. When you're looking at someone and you're trying to give a performance, whatever it is, and that actor is giving you the same performance they gave on their close-up, that's what it's about. I've worked with people who'll give it their all for their close-up, then they turn round to you and it's just literally going through the numbers. And that's difficult because you're wanting those little tiny glimmers of emotion, or that little look in the eye that just breaks your heart, or whatever it is that makes you smile, or feel anxious, or at ease. If that's not there, you're then not acting, you're projecting stuff, because you're not feeling it. But we're lucky here because that's what people bring every day. You get the performance, whether it's in the wide shot or the close-up, whether the camera's on you or on them. Everyone will do their utmost to make it real for that moment that you need it. That's why it's great to come to work, because everyone's here to make it better. Everyone's here to have a great time making it, but work hard when you have to and enjoy it and give each other as much support as possible.

"We have some great laughs and chats and highs and lows. Not everyone gets that at work. Not everyone gets that at home! It's special, it's nice. Everyone that comes in always loves it. I don't know anyone who's come in and gone, 'Nah. Hated that'." He laughs. "Well, no one's said that to my face."

Lots of people had told me that Alex was brilliant at the technical side of acting—knowing where the camera is and how to make the shot work. He says it's an aspect that fascinates him and he's always learning. "The crews are great—massively experienced, massively talented. I think people think that shows like this are quite easy, and sometimes with the talent that's around and the experience that's around, it *is* easy, because everyone knows their job inside out. If you need something, it's been thought of. If the blocking's changed on a scene, the DOP's there helping you out. The camera team are constantly talking to you telling you what's happening. I'm fairly technical so I ask lots of questions about the technical stuff, so there's a real working relationship, there's a conversation going on. It's not, 'Stand here, do that'. Everyone has ideas and suddenly we've got this merry-go-round of excitement and energy and you've got a really good, pacy, fast interesting scene and it comes out of people being great at their jobs, across the board. We don't have weak links. The people that turn up here to work just get it, and get on with it. Every day has its different challenge but every day we rise to it. I'm very proud of everyone that works here, it's great."

He also enjoys watching how other actors work, and particularly enjoys working with some of the guest actors. "I recently worked with Nick Woodeson [who played Artem Chernik in 19/9 'Glass Houses' by Elliot Hope and Johanne McAndrew, 19/11 'The Nightmare Before Christmas' by Katie Douglas and 19/15 'Stick Or Twist' by Joe Ainsworth], who's done everything and he's a proper heavyweight as an actor. We just had a great time. He was in bed for most of his time in Holby. If there's a few minutes between shots you can go off to the green room, but Nick would stay in bed and I'd end up sitting on the bed and we'd just be having a chat. People said those scenes were really good, they bought the relationship between Artem and Fletch and you could see they had a fondness for each other, and I think that came from Nick because he was so good he made me focus and relax. I didn't want to drop the ball and let him down—the actors he's worked with over his career, and now he's here with me, a bit of a chancer from Essex. He just made it easy and that's a real talent, to be able to bring the best out of people. He was a fantastic bloke to work with. Over the years I've done lots of different jobs and I've met and been introduced to some proper big names, real Hollywooders, and its been great to meet some of them, but I'm always much more impressed by talent. Watching someone and them selling it to you 100%, that's much nicer."

Bearing in mind that he's interested in the technical side, I asked if he'd ever thought about directing. "A few people have asked me this," he said. "Sometimes I think I would, but other times I think I like to be drip-fed the idea from the director and then react to it. I can just be across my stuff. I really enjoy pulling faces for a living, I love it. Maybe one day I might give directing a go, but I don't wake up in the middle of the night thinking about it. If the opportunity popped up I'd give it some serious thought, but I'm not going to openly pursue it at the minute. And I think if I was ever going to direct a Holby episode I'd probably have to leave first. It would be healthier for everyone."

He loves Holby and would happily stay long-term, but has learned as an actor that the decision might not always be in his hands. "I plan for my contract and try and work hard every day. That's the only control I have over it. So every day, every scene, I've always got a question. I've always got to have an idea. I need to be on top of it. The directors don't get to cast the regulars, we're already here, they inherit us. They get to cast the guests. So I set myself a challenge. I haven't told anyone this ever before. Years ago when I was on *The Bill*, I'd seen cast members who didn't want to do it any more, they were doing it for money. You know people say they're just phoning it in? And I don't ever, *ever* want to phone it in. So I set myself a challenge that what I would hope for at the end of that block is that if the director had had the choice, they would have asked me to do it. So I just try and work as hard as I can, be as helpful and as honest as I can. To hope that that would be the end result. And I think if I've got that in my head it helps keep me working hard.

"I love it and I do get good storylines and all of those things. Simon,

Ollie and Kate are just fantastic people to work for. Their titles say that you work for them, but as people and bosses you work *with* them. The communication's fantastic, open doors all the time. You ask a question, you get an answer. They're on the floor, they're talking about stories, they'll help you out. It's a much more inclusive relationship than you might have had ten or fifteen years ago, where if you saw the producer you'd know you'd screwed up! I think that's anther reason why it works so well here. They're accessible. They're so passionate about it, it equals the passion on the floor and when everyone has that much passion it will always be better. I like being part of that.

"So I'd stay till all my hair falls out and I have a Zimmer frame. Bob Barrett and I sometimes say it would be nice to do a scene where we're made up to be old men with Zimmer frames and just walking round the ward. I'd have a tiny bit of quiff left, just at the front. More like Homer Simpson, I'm thinking."

KAYE WRAGG (ESSIE HARRISON)

We all want happiness, but in a drama I like to see people who are
dysfunctional and struggling with moments of happiness and
moments of absolute despair. – *Kaye Wragg*

In person, Kaye Wragg is very similar to how she comes across as Essie—
warm, funny and very easy to talk to. In her scrubs, she's also very
believable as a nurse, and it's a job she's quite familiar with from previous
roles, including *No Angels*.

"I've played nurses a few times," she says. "When you play a person in
a job you have to have two hats. You have to know who they are as that
person in that job, and then you have to have the personal side to them as
well. Essie was supposed to be the über-nurse. She was the nurse that never
actually moved on because she put all her energy into looking after her
granddad, which was why she was a bank nurse. If I'm in a scene where
I'm not really doing much I try to make myself look really busy, because
that's what she'd be doing. And she has her job as transplant coordinator,
which is a special field but also allows her to almost nurture people. She
very much cares and does really stand up for the underdog. If there's a story
where there's some truth to be found, she'll sniff it out. She's like a dog with
a bone. She's really professional but almost fights against the idea of 'I'm
just here to do my job'. Her grandfather was a fireman who saved people's

lives and he was on a pedestal for her. She was brought up thinking you save people and then he turns out to be a Nazi. It was the biggest betrayal you could ever have and she's never dealt with it."

Before Kaye took the role as Essie, she'd previously had two guest appearances in Holby. "I guested when Patsy Kensit [Faye Byrne] and Duncan Pow [Linden Cullen] were in it [12/15 'Stop All the Clocks' by Rebecca Wojciechowski]. It was brilliant. I had to have a nervous breakdown. I played a nurse whose son had an accident and died, and I had to freak out and smash up Pulses. Linden had to grab me and calm me down. Patsy was amazing, she was such good fun. My two times of guesting here [the other time was 4/26 'Birthday' by Martin Jameson] I walked away thinking that's one of the loveliest jobs I've ever done. Guests say that now, and it really is. It's not fake, it's genuinely a lovely place to be. I've guested a lot on different shows after I had my children and I hated it because it was so nerve-wracking. Some jobs they just got on with it and it was very professional, but you never felt like you were part of it. Then you come here and guest for three days and you feel like you've been on the job for five months. And then you're out. So both times I guested I loved it."

"Then I came back and worked with Bob [Barrett], and after a week I felt like I'd been here forever, because it's just lovely. It helps that we have a rolling stock of the same crew, people who know the show, because it makes it run smoother. You get the odd new person coming through and that's what they do, they mentor and nurture people. They're brave enough to get people in who've never done anything before and give them an opportunity. You just don't get that anywhere else. I do feel very lucky. Why would you want to go? If you're very young and you want to spread your wings and do other things, I get it, but if you're my age it's like the best of both worlds—you get to act, you get to have your life and mix the two together really. We come to work and have a laugh."

Kaye has two daughters, and she says Holby is the perfect job for her. "If you had a chart with boxes to tick, they'd all be ticked for me because I get to act and I get to be Mum, because I live close by so I can go home every night. If I have days off or scenes off it means I get time with my family. Before that I was constantly living in hotels in Leeds, in Liverpool. When you're an actor and you're not in something regular you have the stress of worrying when the next job's going to be, but when you're away you're missing your family. Here there's a great crew, great cast, everybody's lovely on the fifth floor. They are your family, and if you have any issues they'll help you out. Like on Wednesday my daughter is in a play, so they rejigged a bit so I could leave early. You wouldn't really get that on any other job. So to be a working mum in this environment is incredible, and regardless of how tough and tiring it is, there are so many advantages to it. This is the perfect time of my life because I'm really happy to stay and enjoy seeing what they can do with that character. With this job we sign for a year and we have no idea what's going to happen to our character. So there's excitement and nervousness and you have to trust that they've got ideas. They have the bigger picture. All you can do is make the script work."

One of the things that clearly works is the on-screen and off-screen bond she has with Bob Barrett, who plays Sacha Levy. "From the minute we stepped on the floor together we had an instant rapport," she says, and tells a story of when her husband [actor Jamie Darling] came home nineteen years ago and said he'd met "the loveliest actor" while he was working on a job. "Bob had his eldest child, who was then a baby, in a green room with the rugby on TV silently because the baby was sleeping. My husband was doing a different job in the studios and was searching for this rugby match, and sat with Bob. They watched this rugby match in silence so they didn't disturb the baby. My husband never stopped talking about how lovely this man was. When I got the audition to play Essie I thought I'd better watch Holby, and my husband said, 'That's the man I sat and watched rugby with all those years ago!', and it was Bob. I said that's the man who's going to be playing opposite me. I told Bob on the first day and he remembered the whole incident—he just remembers everything. And we've never stopped talking since. I've met his family, he's met mine. We are extensions of Essie and Sacha really, because we get on set and we laugh and we joke. We never really discuss the scene, we just do it and it's there."

Kaye feels that Essie and Sacha are soul mates. "Sacha is the love of her life and she's the love of his life and we were really devastated when they broke us up because we love working together," she says. "Despite their faults, you look at them and you go, 'They should just be together'. But the writers decided there would be more weight in separating them and giving them air. They're there for each other through their darkest times. Essie was there through his depression, which kind of came out of nowhere, but it was partly because he can't be with her. No matter what happens between Essie and Sacha and who they're with, Bob and I both think it's important to maintain the link between the two of them because that hasn't gone. It's what would happen in life—you always say there's the one that got away, and I think that's what we want to play. We want to keep that little spark alive, which we beg them to write all the time. They're far too linked, so they can't be out of each other's lives. She knows him so well. They're always there for each other, but they can't be together right now."

When Essie and Sacha were first together as a couple, I felt that Essie was acting a little disapproving of him, rather like Chrissie had done. "I never understood that," Kaye says. "I didn't watch it when Sacha and Chrissie were together so I didn't know what relationship they had. Originally I was only going to be here for five months. But then Niamh McGrady [Mary-Claire Carter] was going away to do a second series of *The Fall*, so to cover that time gap they brought in Essie temporarily. Then they liked the relationship between Essie and Sacha, but they hadn't planned that far ahead. When I got the last script and it said Essie was going to Germany but was potentially coming back, I got excited thinking I might be coming back. I think the way they wrote it was that because of Essie's Nazi grandfather and Sacha's Jewish family, she wasn't sure if she could have a relationship with this man, in case she damaged him. While she was away he'd stopped replying to her emails and she had a fling, so when she came back she didn't know what that meant about how she felt about him. I think what they were trying to unlock was that Essie's not in control, not sure of who she is and what she wants. I feel that her smile and everything is just bravado and at some point it's going to hit her like a steam train and she'll have to deal with everything. That's how I play her, though I don't know if those things will ever be addressed on the show. I think with Sacha she pushed him away, and blamed him for being too nice when she felt she didn't deserve it. She lets life control her rather than be in control of her life."

Kaye has strong views about Essie's struggle to have a child of her own. At the time I spoke to her there were rumours that her character would get pregnant at some point in series 19, but Kaye wasn't sure it was the right way to go. "I think there are so many people who watch the show who've been in that situation and never got the happy ending," she says. "I err on the side of not having fairytale endings for characters because I think that's too easy. I think drama and angst and worry and concern continue through the things we hate with our own lives because it's not perfect and we don't get what we want. And sometimes if you get what you want, where does that leave the story? We all want happiness, but in a drama I like to see people who are dysfunctional and struggling with moments of happiness and moments of absolute despair, because that's what I've been through and around me it's happening all the time. We don't always get what we want and it's nice in drama to see somebody face those issues."

The Keller family has been a very tight-knit unit of Kaye, Bob Barrett and David Ames for the last three years. "I wasn't sure whether they were going to make Dom and Essie enemies to start with," Kaye says. "When Zosia and Arthur were there and it was the three of them, I was very much more adult, though when I started they told me Essie had a wicked sense of humour, very dry and witty. Then when they went they almost lowered Essie's humour to be able to have that silly banter. It's lovely."

She really enjoys her scenes with David Ames, particularly those little moments when Essie and Dominic are sitting at the nurses' station on Keller gossiping and making each other laugh. "David and I love it when they let us sit side by side at the nurses' station and do our thing. It's very dry and droll and Essie and Dom wind each other up a treat, but they have a fantastic connection because they can be really rude to each other, really funny to each other, and they know buttons they can press to wind each other up. And they have silly little games like deciding who's handsome, who's not. There's no threat with each other, so they can really push over the line. We regard ourselves as the two Muppets, the ones that sit on the balcony. We love those scenes. Certain directors don't like us sitting down to do that, they want to move us around, but we beg them to let us do our little Muppet moment. It's a bit of light relief.

"When I come here I mess around so much. At home I'm a mum, I've got millions of things to do and I'm very grown up and very responsible. I come here and I don't have to do anything apart from my job. On set the banter is ridiculously childish or extremely rude, but we're allowed to do that. Sometimes the directors have to shout at us to get us to focus! I would rather work under those conditions. When they say, 'Action', we're ready, the focus is there. It's a balance of doing very long days and keeping sane."

Like Alex Walkinshaw, Kaye is very inspired by the guest artists who come to work on Holby. "They bring a brand new energy to every day. We get such great guests. There are newcomers and you think, wow they're going to be brilliant in their career, and we get some of the older people coming in that I grew up watching. I had Julian Glover, who played my granddad [16/30 'My Name Is Joe' by Johanne McAndrew and Elliot Hope, and 16/31 'No Apologies' by Anna McPartlin]. I nearly fell off my chair when I found out he was playing my granddad, because I grew up watching him in films, and it was just magical for me to do those scenes with him. So those guest actors keep it fresh and energised."

BERENA: A SURPRISING LOVE STORY

We were well into that story without ever having anticipated what a huge story it would turn into. – Simon Harper

"It had come up in a story conference that Serena could have a gay relationship," story producer Kate Hall told me. "I said to the writers, 'Please tell me you're not trying to tell a shocking coming-out story'. This is a love story. A surprising love story for someone who hasn't been lucky in love."

When Serena first appeared in Series 14 she was fierce and rather scary, but as time went on she started showing the cheekier, funnier side of her personality. The standalone episode in Series 16 (16/13 'Self Control' by Rebecca Wojciechowski) really saw the flowering of Serena's character, when we saw her getting drunk with Ric Griffin and shamelessly flirting with random men. The episode also saw her finally getting over her no-hoper husband, Edward. Edward, played by Aden Gillett, was a womanising alcoholic and it was clear to everyone but Serena that she was too good for him.

"All of a sudden people started to relate to Serena because she's going through things women our age are going through," Kate Hall says. Not only was Serena unlucky in love, she also had to deal with caring for her mother who had dementia. The storyline with Adrienne (beautifully played by Sandra Voe) further raised Serena's profile in the affections of the fans.

Relationship-wise, Edward was followed by a swift fling with one of the hospital management and with police officer Robbie, who started hanging around AAU. Robbie seemed to be Mr Right and he and Serena were ready to move in together until 18/28 ('Prioritise the Heart' by Julia Gilbert), when Robbie balked at the idea of sharing domestic bliss with Serena's nephew Jason.

It was something of a risk for Serena's next romance to be with another woman. The woman had to be very special, and in Jemma Redgrave Holby had the perfect person.

Bernie's very first appearance in 18/17 ('A Partnership, Literally' by Andy Bayliss) was as a patient, and she spent the entire episode horizontal. She still managed to radiate charisma. We learned that she had a husband and also a close personal colleague in Afghanistan who sent her flowers. When this close personal colleague, Alex (Heather Peace) appeared in person in 18/28 ('Prioritise the Heart' by Julia Gilbert), we discovered that although Bernie was married to a man, she was deeply in love with Alex.

The attraction between Serena and Bernie was set up in a subtle but very deliberate way. "We knew where we were going with that the moment Bernie joined," executive producer Oliver Kent explained. "We started putting it in the edit. We would cut in looks between them to let the audience think they were spotting it before we meant them to, which is what we always do. It's quite funny when you see people's reactions to something they think we didn't mean them to spot, like lingering looks at the end of the scene. It works a treat."

I feel so manipulated now, although I didn't spot that things were becoming romantic between the two of them till episode 34 ('The Sky is Falling' by Andy Bayliss). Before that I'd happily accepted the pair as supportive work colleagues, and that in itself was a refreshing thing to see on TV—two high-powered women collaborating and helping each other (after some initial teething problems) rather than being bitchy and competitive. It also made the ensuing romance seem more natural, as it grew out of friendship and mutual respect.

When Serena was upset on the day of Arthur's funeral (18/36) it was Bernie who comforted her, and by episode 41 I was noting that they were holding each other's gaze a little longer than usual. A couple of weeks later (18/44), Bernie's son Cameron (Nic Jackman) noticed that Bernie looked at Serena the way she used to look at Alex. I felt that this came as news to Bernie—but once Cameron had put it into words, she realised it was true.

The turning point came in the aftermath of the shocking incident when Fletch was stabbed. Bernie and Serena fought to save his life in the operating theatre, and as they sat outside the theatre exhausted, they kissed. Catherine Russell told *What's On TV* in August 2016 about the kiss: "It was the day after the Brexit vote and both Jemma and I had spent the entire day bursting into tears and being really genuinely upset. That was the very last scene being shot on that day, so we were both genuinely knackered, upset and deeply stressed out and we did the read-through for that scene sitting on the floor and the director said, 'That's it, don't move, do it like that'. So while there are not very many silver linings to the Brexit vote I can say that that was one of them – I think the scene benefited from that because there was no acting required, we were just really p***** off!" As for the kiss itself, Catherine said on Twitter, "We didn't need 2 prepare, if we don't know how 2 kiss at our age we're in trouble."

There was also a lovely scene (18/48) where Serena 'came out' to a comatose Fletch, trying out how 'Serena Campbell... lesbian' sounded. Fletch later revealed he'd heard every word.

Fans were delighted at the development, but not long after that it looked like the partnership was only going to be short-lived, as Bernie seemed to get cold feet and accepted a job abroad, leaving Serena distraught.

This plot development was written around Jemma Redgrave requesting some time off, but Simon Harper was keenly aware that a lot of fans were now strongly invested in the 'Berena' storyline. He didn't want them to feel they were being let down by Holby succumbing to the tired TV trope that lesbian relationships never fare well on mainstream TV. "I ask myself whether I should say things on Twitter to reassure them, or not?" he told me. ("Not," muttered Oliver Kent). "I'm really conscious of them assuming that we're going to do wrong by a lesbian story, that we would punish them and not let them be happy, and I don't want them thinking that."

Catherine Russell was also clear about the show's responsibility to get the story right. "From the perspective of a lesbian viewer, there's so little out there on regular TV that they can look at and go, 'That represents me, there I am,'" she told *What's On TV*. "I think for those people it will be really quite significant. Over the years, gay men have had role models on TV shows, including Holby, but there are very, very few gay women. So I think and hope there will be a good deal of support. At the end of the day, love is love."

Holby fan Elayna Thornton-Reeves can thoroughly relate to the story. "If there is one thing I had always been sure about in my life it is the fact that I was gay," she says. "I think a lot of us are hoping that the story with Bernie and Serena ends up in marriage." She thinks that the maturity of the relationship is realistic. "I have seen a lot of people complain on social media that we have not seen a lot of them being close to each other, sharing moments of kissing or cuddling. In reality these are two very professional women who know how to keep their work and personal lives separate." Even the tragedy of Serena's daughter dying has only reinforced the bond between the two, according to Elayna. "They have found each other at a time in their lives which neither of them expected. Tragedy has intervened at the moment and they are struggling to hold things together both at home and professionally, but deep down in their hearts they know how they truly feel. If you really understand how to love someone you can get through anything together."

Another Berena fan, Beth Mason, agrees. "The moment I heard about Holby having a middle-aged same sex relationship I was overjoyed. The moment Bernie Wolfe met Serena Campbell you just knew it was going to be something special and Holby did not disappoint. The impact it's had on everyone is incredible. Same sex relationships weren't something that was widely seen on prime time television shows such as Holby. It has had a incredibly positive impact especially for the LGBT+ community.

For me what makes it so special is that it's middle-aged women and that it is accepted. It's so important to acknowledge that same sex relationships happen no matter what gender or age you are. It brings me joy and hope to see that whatever curveballs are thrown at them their relationship survives no matter what. The sheer strength and love and the promise of hope involved in the relationship matters so much. I look up to this relationship and it gives me so much positivity and it reminds me of strength we should all have when it comes to love. I want to personally thank the writers of *Holby City*, Jemma Redgrave and Catherine Russell for believing in this storyline, for acting it out perfectly and for giving it a voice."

Berena has had a significant impact on the lives of a lot of women. Hannah Watts explains how it gave her strength at a difficult time in her life. "At the start of the Berena storyline, when they finally got together, I had been going through a dark time. I didn't think I could carry on with life and I was admitted to hospital after an attempt on my own life. Watching them and the storyline really inspired me to accept myself and my sexuality. I was already semi-out as bisexual, but watching these two older women find happiness and acceptance in themselves helped me find my own acceptance in myself. Watching Berena got me through those times. I owe so much to Catherine and Jemma and I cannot thank them enough for all the support and awareness they have spread with the Berena storyline."

Executive producer Simon Harper was very mindful of the story's impact when I spoke to him about it in May 2017. Holby staff knew by then, though the fans didn't, that Jemma Redgrave was about to leave. Catherine Russell would be returning from her sabbatical as Serena, but without Bernie.

"We never anticipated what a phenomenon it would turn into," he said. "And the Berena fandom—I'd never anticipated that whatsoever. I perhaps hadn't appreciated the issue of under-representation of gay women of that age. To me I'd just thought of it as a great story for Catherine's character and it just took off from there and I never thought it would have this response.

"Then Catherine asked me, quite understandably and deservedly after five years, if she could have a nine-month break. Then of course Jemma is leaving, so Bernie will disappear off the screen and then Serena will return without Bernie. When Bernie leaves she references going to join Serena in the south of France, where she's recuperating and getting her joie de vivre back in a vineyard. After the trauma centre in AAU is closed because of cuts, Bernie revisits her first love, which is military trauma medicine, but seeing Serena en route. So she'll be spending some time with Serena, but then Serena will come back on her own. That's the vagaries of continuing drama, and it's something we have limited control over. When actors come and go you just regard it as a creative opportunity, and the Berena relationship has been characterised by the movements of these busy actresses.

"You'll have noticed when Serena and Bernie first kissed, Bernie disappeared for weeks, almost to the frustration of fans. It was really interesting and instructive to me how that whole angst springs up that we're going to punish these gay characters because apparently there's this precedent for it, as a lot of gay female fans see it. I don't know why everybody thinks we're going to punish these characters. What was really happening was that Jemma wanted to have a break and go and do something else, which we'd always said we could do when we first hired her. When an actor asks for a break you write around it and we turned it into an opportunity. Her return became such a massive payoff for the Berena audience."

And to the relief of worried Berena fans, series producer Kate Hall told *Digital Spy* in August 2017, "We will return to [the Berena story] as and when the actors feel ready to return, but suffice to say, that's a love story that remains."

THE DEATH OF DIGBY:
WALKING ARTHUR HOME

Everyone brought their A game. Everyone stepped
it up and did the best they could for it. – *Bob Barrett*

One of the most memorable episodes in recent years has been the one
that dealt with the death of Arthur Digby (18/35 'I'll Walk You Home'
by Andy Bayliss).

I was invited to a screening of that and the preceding episode (18/34
'The Sky Is Falling,' also by Andy Bayliss) at the BBC bar at Elstree
Studios, but Oliver Kent sent me a link so I could watch it before then.
My dad had recently died and, knowing how powerful the episode was,
Ollie perhaps thought I might like to get my snot-crying out of the way
in the comfort of my own home.

He wasn't wrong. I've watched episode 35 lots of times now and been
an emotional wreck during the last fifteen minutes every time. I'm not
the only one. Episode 35 got the best audience appreciation index ever,
and viewers were united in their praise for how beautifully the death of
a well-loved character was handled.

The screening at the BBC bar was attended by Rob Ostlere (Arthur
Digby), Eleanor Fanyinka (Morven Digby) and David Ames (Dominic
Copeland), as well as executive producer Oliver Kent, story producer

Kate Hall, Andy Bayliss who wrote the episodes, Paulette Randall who directed them, production manager Ali Liddle and others. By the end of the second episode as the screen faded to black, everyone was in tears. There was a feeling in the room that something very special had been created, and even now Ali Liddle can get emotional when talking about the scenes of Arthur dying. "I couldn't go down to set when we shot that, because even though it was Rob and I knew he was all right, and it wasn't even the last thing we shot with him, it was still quite upsetting," she says. "And I thought, 'If I'm that upset and I'm working on it…'"

The storyline came about when Rob Ostlere told the show's bosses he felt it was time to move on. "It was completely and utterly gutting," Oliver Kent said. "So we had to make sure we had a really stonking exit story for him." Kate Hall agrees, saying that Rob is "a fabulous actor, the kind of guy you could grow up on a show and keep going. I'd have kept Rob for ever and ever if I had a choice." Given that Rob's decision was firmly made, Kate also felt that British television didn't deal well with death, so here was a great opportunity to do something "brilliant and bold."

When the idea of Digby dying was pitched to Rob, his reaction was initially very emotional, so much so that the producers reassured him that Digby didn't have to die, they could do another exit storyline instead. But Rob thought it was an important story to tell and wanted to do it.

Ellie Fanyinka remembers that she was sitting in the sun in Green Park in London when she got a phone call from Rob. "He'd just had a meeting with Simon [Harper] and he called me and said 'They've told me what's going to happen and how I'm going to go'. I'd known he was going to go for a while, but when he told me I cried and I cried and I cried. In that moment I knew I was losing Arthur Digby. It sounds ridiculous, but you spend so many hours a day with that character. Both of us were crying."

Bob Barrett (Sacha) felt the same. "Camilla [Arfwedson] said 'I've got a text from Rob saying Arthur's going to have cancer and he's going to die.' And I said it must be a wind-up, because they wound each other up all the time. And then we saw him and sat down with him and he told us that it was true, and even then we got upset."

Kate Hall really wanted to do an episode that told the story from the point of view of a dying person. The hallucinatory scenes which take place in Arthur's head are a break of format for the usually realistic Holby, and Kate said she initially thought of doing the whole episode in that way. The writer, Andy Bayliss, wanted to frame those scenes with other action, and Kate believes that was the right way to tell the story in the end. "Andy's an ex-script editor, so he understands structure," she says. "The more I watch that episode, the more it feels like a feature film, there's so much going on in it."

Andy says the storyline was planned for a long time and his focus for episodes 34 and 35 was "how to dramatise how someone like Arthur might deal with this final stage and how best to show how those around him who loved him would cope."

Morven, Dominic and Zosia—as Digby's wife and two best friends—were the centre of the story, but Andy also wanted the 'parental' figures of Sacha, Ric, Serena, Hanssen and Jac to be involved, so Digby had the chance to say goodbye to everyone who'd been significant to him. This was the reason he wove the episode around Digby trying to piece together his feelings about his hospital 'family'. It was also the reason for including the dance sequence, which Andy told me had been inspired by a real-life incident he'd read about. He then had to weave in the guest stories, so they would have the most impact without detracting from the main focus on Arthur's story and would feel integral to the plot. The character of Alison [Lee's wife, played by Elizabeth Cadwallader] was brought back because she had chemistry with Dominic and "would give him something else to worry about other than Arthur."

Rob and the story team worked with consultant oncologist Dr Bruce Sizer to ensure that the medical story was accurate and believable. Dr Sizer said that, "Arthur's story became quite complicated and reflects the way that unfortunately melanoma can behave". Rob said that, while it was one thing to understand the medical aspects of the story, the challenge was to understand what it was like to go through the illness. "You just have to do your best to represent it." He said he talked to friends who'd been affected by cancer but mainly followed what was written in the scripts, because they were so well researched. The story received the approval of the charity Melanoma UK, whose founder Gillian Nuttall said, "The melanoma storyline in Holby has certainly done a good job in raising awareness of the disease. Our helpline has seen an increase in calls from people who otherwise might not have paid attention to a skin change. Rob Ostlere's portrayal has resonated with a number of melanoma sufferers."

The episodes were both directed by Paulette Randall MBE, who says she'll never forget the experience. They were the first episodes she ever directed for Holby, and before she agreed to do it she wasn't really aware of Arthur Digby as a character and his story up to that point. "The one thing that hit me once I'd read the scripts and I'd watched some back episodes to see a bit more about his journey, was that I have to absolutely honour this character and I have to absolutely give him the right send-off that will honour him," she says. "I thought, 'Okay, this is very precious and it means an awful lot to a lot of people, and I need to allow them the space to mourn and grieve as well as celebrate'. So that was paramount."

She was able to talk to Andy Bayliss about how he envisaged the episodes. An early draft of the script started episode 35 with a dream sequence, with Digby on the roof, looking down at all of the regular cast walking out of the hospital. Chantelle is also there and she calls out and asks if he's coming. Paulette felt that doing it that way would signal to the audience that something was really wrong. "As it is now, up till quite late on you're still optimistic for him," she says. "Then the last part just rips your heart and your guts out."

Ali Liddle says that it was complicated working out who would be at Arthur's bedside at his death, and who would be in the dance sequence. "Ideally we wanted people from all three wards in the dance but we couldn't do it, because some people were busy shooting with another unit, so in some cases people mentioned the dance earlier on but never actually appeared in it."

The dance scene lightened the whole episode, providing contrast to the heart-rending scenes at the end. It was important to everyone involved in the story that it wasn't all doom and gloom. "It's all about balance," Oliver Kent says. "If you're going to kill a character as popular as Arthur then there has to be something funny going on, or something triumphant, or something warm and hopeful at the same time."

Rob Ostlere told *What's On TV* that, "Arthur's always been very closed-minded about certain things and, suddenly, he opened up emotionally and revealed a different side to himself. Arthur developed a real sense of freedom through realising what's important about life...and what's important to him."

David Ames remembers the scene with Arthur and Dominic in the store room. "I'd gone off to have a moment and he comes in and sits with me and says, 'I think I'm meant to be here, and I just want things to be normal.' That was my very last scene with Rob and the poignant thing for me was seeing them laugh together and the hope that was there, and how that gets dashed by the end."

Paulette Randall particularly liked the scene where Arthur collapses in Hanssen's office. "What was gorgeous about that was that you saw this usually quite reserved man, Hanssen, and you absolutely knew how much he loved Arthur, there was no question. That was just beautiful to have. He played it wonderfully. They both did. It's a joy to work with such talent. It's great."

Ellie Fanyinka says the tears that she shed during her final speech to Arthur at his bedside and in the dreamlike sequences were real, and she'd even cried reading the script on her phone when she got it. "The language was quite poetic. It required work," she says. "I made it quite specific and I made sure I was really talking to Arthur in that last moment. What I was saying was quite powerful, I had to be doing something to him, like everything I said to him had to be active. So I really worked on that and made sure the intention behind each thing I was saying was specific and real. I didn't want to do the episode or the writing a disservice, and I certainly didn't want to do Rob a disservice."

"Ellie was amazing," Bob Barrett says. "That speech was just extraordinary. And everyone brought their A game, everyone stepped it up and did the best they could for it. It was written beautifully. There wasn't a misstep along the way, really. And I miss him. I still see Rob and I know he's happy, but I miss Arthur. Sacha misses Arthur. I'm glad they remind the audience about him a lot, because I think it's right. Someone who was on our watch—with all that potential—died, and that's something that will colour Holby forever, I think."

Bob's favourite part of the episode, and the bit that makes a lot of people cry (if they aren't crying already) is when Zosia gets the phone call about Arthur and collapses in tears and Jac rushes to comfort her. Camilla Arfwedson says that it was filmed really quickly, because Rosie Marcel's daughter wasn't well and Rosie had to dash off to pick her up. Camilla says she'd been planning to work on the scene on her own, but in the end there wasn't time. "It worked out quite well, because I didn't want to over-think it. It's so easy to emote and one tear creeps beautifully down your face, but is that really what happens?" she says. "Zosia had been bottling it up for so long and trying to plough on and put on a brave face. She was in complete denial about everything and focusing on her work. She doesn't think anything's really wrong, she's going to fix him, he'll get the stent, everything's going to be fine, all that stuff. And when she fails at that, the one…" At this point her voice breaks and she has to make an effort not to cry. "Oh gosh, it's making me emotional just talking about it. Ugh! The one person who she had a genuine friendship with… She just crumbles. I said to the director, 'I want her to feel like she's been shot'. The information just floors her, instantly floors her. I don't think we really even rehearsed it because Rosie had to run off. We did it in one take, and that was it. It was great. That's when it's really cool here. Paulette said, 'That was all I needed'. We could have done it three or five times, spent time on it, talked about it some more, but we didn't. We just did it. I was quite surprised by the response to it actually. It was really nice how people responded to it."

FROM THE SCRIPT OF 18/35 'I'LL WALK YOU HOME BY ANDY BAYLISS

35/50. INT. KELLER. RECOVERY ROOM – NIGHT (22:00)

MORVEN has just made it to ARTHUR's side. He lies unconscious, Diamorphine controlling his symptoms… There is music playing – the same piano music that ARTHUR could hear.

HANSSEN behind her. DOMINIC at ARTHUR's side – it all seems so surreal.

                    MORVEN
          I'm here now Arthur.

But she's struggling with it all... She looks to HANSSEN who passes
her the medals.

But even HANSSEN is finding it hard to disguise his concern.

                    DOMINIC
          They said he should have some
          music. This was on there, I don't
          know if...

                    MORVEN
          Thank you.

HANSSEN looks to DOMINIC, smiles – they should leave her.

And we pull back revealing that most of AAU and Keller (as many as
possible) have begun gathering...

                    MORVEN
          I don't know what it is you think
          you're doing?

CUT TO:

35/51. INT. AAU. VICTORIAN CORRIDOR/WAITING AREA – NIGHT

ARTHUR sitting in his scrubs facing MORVEN.

                    MORVEN
          You're supposed to be telling me
          which flats we can't afford to

rent. Who's going to stop me
painting the kitchen that horrible
rust colour I like now?

ARTHUR smiles.

CUT TO:

35/52. INT. KELLER. RECOVERY ROOM – NIGHT (22:01)

MORVEN at his side, she's struggling – ARTHUR not moving, seems so
lifeless – she's not sure what to say:

> MORVEN
> We were right about Ms Marias. We
> fixed her... I fixed her. And that
> feeling was so good Arthur. So good
> because it reminded me of you...

As she summons her strength.

> MORVEN
> Reminded me of what you loved so
> much. Being the difference for
> people.

And now the tears are coming.

> MORVEN
> So, I'll keep going. I'll keep
> going for you – and every time I
> get that feeling – that someone is
> better, that I did good in the
> world... I'll know it's because
> you're there with me.

MORVEN trying to stem the tide now.

> MORVEN
> I don't know if it sunk in just how
> much you mean to so many people
> here – if you really knew. But you
> gave a bit of yourself to all of us
> Arthur Digby... to Dom and to
> Zosia, Malick, Sacha – so many
> people Arthur... And I know you
> kept a small bit of you back, just
> for me...

CUT TO:

35/53. INT. AAU. VICTORIAN CORRIDOR/WAITING ROOM – NIGHT

ARTHUR standing now...

> MORVEN
> So thank you. Because I'll never
> forget that. I love you more than
> you can imagine. More than I ever
> thought possible. So you're not
> going, not entirely.

He looks down at his feet – sees that he has his shoes on. He has shoes! He looks up and he's alone, but he smiles...because it's okay...

> MORVEN (V.O)
> And I only hope you know, that I
> tried to give you back as much as
> you gave to me. More.

CUT TO:

35/54. INT. KELLER. RECOVERY ROOM – NIGHT (22:03)

As MORVEN notices the medals on the side. She picks them up. Lays them on his chest. Strokes his face.

> MORVEN
> Don't be scared...

And as if summoning every last ounce of strength he has – he lets her know that he heard every last word – he squeezes her hand... she feels it...

> MORVEN
> I know.

Long beat as if she's listening to him – she nods, tears streaming – can feel him going. Just about gets the words out:

> MORVEN
> I'll walk you home, Arthur.

And, as if that's all he needed to hear, his hand releases again... And he's gone.

The machine signals his end.

CUT TO:

35/55. INT. KELLER. RECOVERY ROOM/LIFT LOBBY – NIGHT (22:03)

The noise of the machine continuing... Pick up the various reactions, heads drop, all comforting each other (ESSIE and SACHA, SERENA and FLETCH etc) as they hear that familiar sound – now so poignant – as one of their own is taken from them...

As RIC goes to a numb DOMINIC, DOMINIC moves away from him – walks out – his phone to his ear...

CUT TO:

35/56. INT. DARWIN. CENTRAL NURSES' STATION – NIGHT (22:03)

Sound of machine continues...

We're with JAC as she sees ZOSIA taking a phone call from DOMINIC... And JAC knows exactly what it is... Heads for her.

ZOSIA puts the phone down, sits on a bed and just breaks – tears flooding from her, as JAC takes her in her arms, embraces her...

GUY comes into shot – sees the two of them together and we're left wondering at the ambiguity of it – is he saddened that's not him, or did he have a hand in pushing these two together...

Either way, he takes his leave.

CUT TO:

35/57. INT. KELLER. RECOVERY ROOM – NIGHT (22:04)

The sound of the machine reverberates

The team (as many as possible; HANSSEN, RIC, SERENA, SACHA, ESSIE, FLETCH) have moved in to support MORVEN and stand at ARTHUR's bedside like a guard of honour.

They watch as MORVEN summons the strength, switches it off... All is quiet.

She stands by his side. Not sure what to do. Her soulmate gone – her world forever altered... As we go out, for the very last time, on the deceased:

Doctor Arthur Digby.

END OF EPISODE

ACKNOWLEDGEMENTS

You'll have read throughout this book that everybody says Holby is a special place, and it really is. I thoroughly enjoyed being a little part of it for a while and getting to meet such interesting people. Even though everybody is incredibly busy and the pace never lets up, people were very generous in taking the time to talk to me.

Oliver Kent, Simon Harper and Kate Hall were encouraging and enthusiastic about the idea of a book from the start, and they couldn't have been more helpful. Lucy Roper organised things beautifully so I got to talk to all the people I wanted to and poke my nose around the building.

Ali Liddle took me to visit the sets while filming was in progress (and thanks to to all the people working on those sets who didn't mind having a nosy member of the public hanging round, and even took time out to explain things to me). Ali is also due massive thanks for supplying the wonderful photos in this book.

Huge thanks for their time and their kindness to David Ajao, David Ames, James Anderson, Camilla Arfwedson, Helen Ashley, Bob Barrett, Andy Bayliss, Robi Borgonovo, Hayley Cameron, John Cannon, Keren Coleman, Sarah Creasey, Matt Denison, Ellie Fanyinka, Nick Fisher, Hannah Goraya, Lynn Grant, Guy Henry, Patrick Homes, Jo Houtmeyers, Jaye Jacobs, George Kyriakides, Rosie Marcel, Joe McFadden, Lee Mead, John Michie, Mike Narduzzo, Rob Platt, Hugh Quarshie, Paulette Randall MBE, Jemma Redgrave, Catherine Russell, Lisa Spencer-Blackshaw, Liz Stoll, Lina Stroud, Megan Thomas, Christian Vit, Alex Walkinshaw, Lorna Whittaker and Kaye Wragg.

Thank you also to Beth Mason, Elayna Thornton-Reeves and Hannah Watts for sharing their thoughts about the Berena storyline.